GRAMMAR DIMENSIONS 2

PLATINUM EDITION

WORKBOOK

Cheryl Benz
Miami-Dade Community College

Ann Roemer

HH **Heinle & Heinle**
Thomson Learning

Australia • Canada • Denmark • Japan • Mexico • New Zealand
Philippines • Puerto Rico • Singapore • Spain • United Kingdom • United States

Acquisitions Editor: Eric Bredenberg
Senior Developmental Editor: Amy Lawler
Production Editor: Michael Burggren
Senior Marketing Manager: Charlotte Sturdy
Manufacturing Coordinator: MaryBeth Hennebury
Composition: The Clarinda Company
Project Management: Emily Autumn
Cover Design: Hannus Design Associates

Photos: page 15, © Rhoda Sidney/PhotoEdit; page 29, courtesy of H. Armstrong Roberts; page 60, Stock, Boston, Inc.; page 86, courtesy of Red Cross; page 150, courtesy of United Nations Library; page 152, courtesy of Stock, Boston, Inc.

For permission to use material from this text, contact us:
web   www.thomsonrights.com
fax   1-800-730-2215
phone   1-800-730-2214

Heinle & Heinle Publishers
20 Park Plaza
Boston, MA 02116

UK/EUROPE/MIDDLE EAST:
Thomson Learning
Berkshire House
168-173 High Holborn
London, WC1 V 7AA, United Kingdom

ASIA (excluding Japan):
Thomson Learning
60 Albert Street #15-01
Albert Complex
Singapore 189969

AUSTRALIA/NEW ZEALAND:
Nelson/Thomson Learning
102 Dodds Street
South Melbourne
Victoria 3205 Australia

JAPAN:
Thomson Learning
Palaceside Building, 5F
1-1-1 Hitotsubashi, Chiyoda-ku
Tokyo 100 0003, Japan

CANADA:
Nelson/Thomson Learning
1120 Birchmount Road
Scarborough, Ontario
Canada M1K 5G4

SPAIN:
Thomson Learning
Calle Magallanes, 25
28015-Madrid
Espana

LATIN AMERICA:
Thomson Learning
Seneca, 53
Colonia Polanco
11560 México D.F. México

ISBN: 0-8384-0274-7

This book is printed on acid-free recycled paper.

Printed in the United States of America
1 2 3 4 5 6 7 8 9 04 03 02 01 00

TOEFL® is a registered trademark of Educational Testing Service (ETS). This product is not endorsed or approved by ETS.

CONTENTS

UNIT 1

SIMPLE PRESENT

Habits, Routines, and Facts

Read about the students in their writing class. Underline the verbs that tell about habits (things they do again and again, sometimes without realizing it) or routines (things they do regularly). The first one has been done for you as an example.

Writing is my favorite class because of my classmates. Even though they <u>work</u> hard to improve their writing, they like to have fun, too. Raul and Suzette study the hardest. They always listen carefully to the directions and raise their hands when they have a question. They are good students, and they try to encourage other students. Jean Marc is my best friend in the class. He always helps me with my writing assignments. Before I rewrite my papers, I always ask him to read them. He helps me see my mistakes.

There is only one student who doesn't participate in class—Yaniv. He always interrupts the teacher and whispers to other students. Sometimes he eats and drinks in class. Besides that, he never pays attention, and he hardly ever does his assignments.

Write five sentences about habits or routines of a good student. Then write five sentences about the habits or routines of a poor student.

A GOOD STUDENT

1. _____
   _____

2. _____
   _____

3. _____
   _____

4. _____
   _____

5. _____
   _____

A POOR STUDENT

6. _____
   _____

7. _____
   _____

8. _____
   _____

9. _____
   _____

10. _____

The following chart lists the responses of some students to a survey. Using the information on the chart, answer the questions below in complete sentences. The first one has been done for you as an example.

Do you . . .	Yes	No
1. discuss politics with native English speakers?	Raul	Yaniv
2. listen to the radio in English?	Valentina	Wan-Yin
3. watch movies or TV in English?	Mohammed	Yaniv
4. speak English at work or school?	Jean Marc Wan-Yin	
5. read English-language newspapers or magazines	Suzette	Yaniv Valentina
6. go to English class every day?	Su-Ling	
7. write letters in English	Suzette Raul	Su-Ling
8. practice English with native speakers?	Roberto	Valentina

1. Who listens to the radio in English?

   Valentina listens to the radio in English.

2. Who writes letters in English?

   _____

3. Who doesn't read English-language newspapers or magazines?

   _____

4. Who doesn't discuss politics with English speakers?

   _____

5. Who doesn't watch movies in English?

   _____

6. Who speaks English at work or at school?

   _____

7. Who goes to English class every day?

   _____

8. Who practices English with native speakers?

_____

9. Who watches movies or TV in English?

_____

10. Who doesn't listen to the radio in English?

_____

▶ **EXERCISE 4**   *(Focus 2, page 2)*

With a partner, take turns asking each other the eight questions from the chart in Exercise 3. Record your partner's short answers below.

▶ **EXAMPLE:**   **You:** *Do you discuss politics with native English speakers?*
   Your partner: *No, I don't.*

   You write: No, he doesn't. _____

Partner's Name _____

1. _____

2. _____

3. _____

4. _____

5. _____

6. _____

7. _____

8. _____

Now find a new partner. Tell your new partner the information you learned from your first partner.

▶ **EXAMPLE:** *Raul doesn't discuss politics with native English speakers.*

Complete the puzzle by writing in the correct form of each missing verb in the numbered sentences at the left. The first one has been done for you as an example.

1. A spider ____has____ eight legs.

2. Sometimes a lizard _____ its color.

3. A parrot _____ up to 50 years.

4. A fish _____ in the ocean.

5. A panda _____ bamboo sprouts.

6. A bird _____ a nest before she lays an egg.

7. A bat _____ at night.

8. A raccoon always _____ its food.

9. A frog _____ flies with its tongue.

10. A dolphin lives in the water, but it _____ air.

11. A bird _____ on her nest after she lays an egg.

```
1.            H A S
2.    _ _ _ N _ _ _
3.        _ I _ _ _
4.    _ _ _ M _
5.      _ A _ _
6.    _ _ _ L _ _
7.            F _ _ _ _
8.      _ A _ _ _ _
9.  _ _ _ _ C _ _ _
10.   _ _ _ T _ _ _
11.         S _ _ _
```

Do you use several different strategies when you learn a different language, or do you depend on only one or two? Read the sentences below. For each, write the adverb of frequency that best describes your habits as you are learning English.

1. I practice saying new words in sentences so I can remember them.

2. I remember new words by drawing pictures of them.

3. I try to speak like native English speakers.

4. I start conversations with native English speakers.

5. I take notes in English class.

6. I read my notes at home.

7. I try to think in English.

8. I look for similarities and differences between English and my language.

9. I ask English speakers to correct my pronunciation.

10. I try to notice my errors when I speak a language.

Rewrite the statements from Exercise 6 as questions. Ask a partner how often he or she uses each of the different strategies. Record the answers.

► EXAMPLE: **You:** *How often do you practice new words in a sentence so you can remember them?*

Your partner: *I sometimes practice new words in sentences.*

You write: _____ She sometimes practices new words in sentences. _____

1. _____

2. _____

3. _____

4. _____

5. _____

6. _____

7. _____

8. _____

9. _____

10. _____

UNIT 2

PRESENT PROGRESSIVE AND SIMPLE PRESENT

Actions and States

▶ **EXERCISE 1**   *(Focus 1, page 20)*

Read the following paragraphs and underline the present progressives and the time expressions that indicate the action is in progress at or around the time of speaking. The first one has been done for you.

Mohammed is an exchange student from Kuwait who's living in Toronto this academic year. His teachers and classmates are worried about him because he looks tired and is acting differently from the way he usually acts. He's usually very outgoing, and he talks and laughs with the other students, both inside the classroom and out. But these days he isn't smiling much. Normally, Mohammed has lunch in the cafeteria, but today he isn't eating there. He often goes outside to smoke a cigarette, but he's not there smoking today.

Finally, someone asked Mohammed what was wrong. Mohammed explained that he is a Muslim (a follower of Islam). In the lunar calendar, it's now the month of Ramadan, so he's fasting.* This month he isn't eating, drinking, or smoking during daylight hours. The purpose of Ramadan is to teach discipline, and fasting teaches compassion for people who are hungry and thirsty.

Everyone at Mohammed's school is glad that he's all right and that he's just trying to be a good Muslim.

*to fast: not to eat

Using the verbs from the list in the present progressive, complete the dialogues about the following pictures. Be careful—some of them are short answers, some are negative, and others need a pronoun (*you, he, she,* etc.).

► Example: <u>Are they taking</u> *a plane to the conference?*

<u>No, they're taking</u> *the train.*

check	punch	type
die	quit	use
file	stand	water
fill	take	wear

1. _____

someone _____
those letters for me? I need them right now.

Yes, Marcia _____.

2. Who _____ my computer?

Dave _____.

3. Jody, _____
those papers for Ms. Baxter?

No, I _____.

Jim _____.

4. That poor plant _____.

I know. That's why I _____ it.

5. _____ in or

_____ out, sir?

I _____ in.

6. Why _____ in line?
It's 7:00, time for the morning shift to begin.
They _____ in.

7. Where _____ out the application
forms?

In the Human Resources office.

8. What _____

for the job interview today?

I _____

my best dress.

9. Why _____ off his tie?
It's 5 o'clock.

10. Why _____ his job?
Because he hates working in that company.

► **EXERCISE 3**   *(Focus 3, page 22)*

Complete the following paragraph by putting the verbs in parentheses in either the simple present *(swim)* or the present progressive *(be + swimming)*, as needed. Follow the example.

Maria is an athlete who __is representing__ (represent) her country in the Olympic Games. She

(1) _____ (run) in the marathon, a twenty-six-mile race. She usually **(2)** _____

(compete) in the triathlon, which means she **(3)** _____ (have) to run 10 kilometers, swim

1/4 mile, and ride a bicycle 25 miles. There's only a month to go before the Olympics, so Maria

(4) _____ (train) hard to prepare. During regular training, she **(5)** _____

(swim) 1500 meters and **(6)** _____ (run) 5 miles, but during this pre-Olympic

training, she **(7)** _____ (swim) less and **(8)** _____ (run) more. She usually

(9) _____ (work) out in the weight room for an hour every day, but this month she

(10) _____ (lift) weights for two hours a day, double her normal time. Cross-country

skiing is part of her winter training, but now that the weather is warmer, she **(11)** _____

(bicycle) and roller blading so that different muscle groups are exercised. Normally, Maria

(12) _____ (be) careful about her diet; she **(13)** _____ (eat) very little fat

and a lot of fruits and vegetables. Now she **(14)** _____ (make) extra sure that she

(15) _____ (eat) plenty of protein for energy. In addition, she **(16)** _____ (try)

to get enough sleep. She **(17)** _____ (be) confident that she'll be prepared, both mentally

and physically, for the Olympics, and she **(18)** _____ (be) proud to be a part of this

great event.

Cut out a picture from a magazine or newspaper. The picture must have exactly two people in it. Also, make sure it includes activities that you can describe using the present progressive. Write a description of what's happening in the photograph.

Your teacher will show several of the photographs to the entire class and read the descriptions. Listen to each description and decide which picture is being described.

▶ EXERCISE 5   *(Focus 4, page 26)*

Complete the following paragraph by putting the verbs in parentheses in either the simple present *(drive)* or the present progressive *(be + driving)*, as needed. Follow the example.

Stewart and Annie _____are_____ (be) college professors. Right now it **(1)** _____

(be) spring break, and they **(2)** _____ (be) on vacation. They usually **(3)** _____

(travel), but this year they **(4)** _____ (stay) home. They can't take a trip because they

(5) _____ (have) too much to take care of. They have to fix things around the house, and

besides, they **(6)** _____ (think) it **(7)** _____ (be) cruel to leave their pets

home alone. They have three indoor cats. They **(8)** _____ (not own) a dog, but their

next-door neighbor moved away and abandoned her dog, an Alaskan Malamute named Keno.

Stewart and Annie **(9)** _____ (take) care of Keno, which **(10)** _____ (not be)

easy, because he **(11)** _____ (be) a big dog and he **(12)** _____ (be) afraid of

people. Their former neighbor, Theresa, abused the dog. As a result, every time Stewart or Annie

(13) _____ (try) to pet Keno or touch him, the dog jumps away and puts his head

down. He **(14)** _____ (think) that they're going to hit him. He **(15)** _____ (not

understand) kindness; he **(16)** _____ (know) only cruelty. Stewart and Annie

(17) _____ (try) to be patient; they **(18)** _____ (treat) Keno with love, hoping

that someday he will trust human beings again. They **(19)** _____ (take) Keno for a walk

every morning and night, and they **(20)** _____ (play) with him in the yard every day.

Out on the street, Keno **(21)** _____ (not know) how to behave, so the couple

(22) _____ (train) him. He (23) _____ (learn) little by little, and he
(24) _____ (begin) to trust them. They say that they (25) _____ (look) for
a home for him, a place where he would have lots of room to run and people who
(26) _____ (love) him. It (27) _____ (seem) to me that Keno already
(28) _____ (belong) to someone who (29) _____ (love) him.

▶ EXERCISE 6   (Focus 5, page 28)

Read the following sentences in the simple present and the present progressive. For each
sentence, check the column that indicates the meaning of the underlined verb. The first
column, state/quality, includes all of the stative verbs (those expressing states or
qualities—not actions).

	STATE/ QUALITY	ACTION/ EXPERIENCE
1. Mark <u>looks</u> terrible today.	_____	_____
2. <u>Do</u> you <u>think</u> he has the flu?	_____	_____
3. Joe <u>is looking up</u> a word in the dictionary.	_____	_____
4. I <u>think</u> this apartment is too small.	_____	_____
5. I'm <u>thinking</u> about moving to a bigger place.	_____	_____
6. Daniel <u>has</u> a brand-new bicycle.	_____	_____
7. I'm <u>having</u> trouble with my car.	_____	_____
8. P.U.! Something in the refrigerator <u>smells</u> awful.	_____	_____
9. Alonzo's at the perfume counter <u>smelling</u> the colognes.	_____	_____
10. <u>Are</u> you <u>having</u> a good time on your vacation?	_____	_____
11. <u>Do</u> you <u>have</u> time to help me?	_____	_____
12. Thank you. I <u>appreciate</u> your help.	_____	_____
13. Another girlfriend?! Who's he <u>seeing</u> now?	_____	_____
14. I <u>don't see</u> the logic of that argument.	_____	_____
15. Cynthia's <u>having</u> problems with her daughter.	_____	_____

Complete the crossword puzzle on the next page. If you need help, ask a classmate or native speaker of English.

```
        L
M U S I C
        N
        G
        O
```

ACROSS

2. Duet, trio, quartet

8. *Carmen* is an example of an _____ .

10. Are you studying the piano _____ the saxophone?

12. Sheep talk

13. Shakespeare infinitive: To _____ or not to _____ .

14. What kind of lightbulbs are you buying, Philips or General Electric? _____ (abbreviation)

15. Help!

16. A repeated sound . . . sound . . . sound . . . sound . . .

19. A private, personal conversation: a _____ à tête

20. Wear: worn : : tear: _____

21. Second letter in the Greek alphabet

22. Same as 17 Down

23. Either: or : : neither: _____

24. She's working on her Ph.D. in Adult _____ (abbreviation)

25. Sugar cane (Spanish)

29. Host of TV program (abbreviation)

30. Finished (Italian)

32. The _____ in the music conservatory are excellent. I'm learning a lot from them.

DOWN

1. 2 Across performs this way
3. Vulgar insult (abbreviation)
4. U.S. government agency that protects the environment (abbreviation)
5. My fault (Latin): _____ culpa
6. Women's underwear
7. Sixth note of the musical scale
9. In my class, we're doing a _____ paper on different historical periods of music.
11. That band is _____ ing a CD with Sony.
13. Soprano: top notes : : bass: _____ notes
15. Past participle of *see*
17. Hours (abbreviation)
18. Opposite of *off*
19. Tuberculosis (abbreviation)
25. U.S. spies work for this government agency
26. Political group in South Africa
27. National Institutes of Health (abbreviation)
28. Past tense of *eat*
30. Faith (Spanish)
31. Same as 10 Across

Unit 3

Talking About the Future

Be Going To and Will

▶ EXERCISE 1   (Focus 1, page 36)

The sentences in the following conversation are about the future. Underline the subject and verb form (*will* or *be going to*) and time expression that indicates the future.

▶ **EXAMPLE:** <u>Will you marry</u> *me, Nancy?* <u>I will love</u> *you* <u>for the rest of my life</u>.

Nancy is engaged to be married. She and her fiancé, Tim, are trying to make their wedding plans, but Nancy's mother doesn't agree with them.

Nancy's mother: Now, I have it all planned, honey. We're going to go shopping for your wedding dress this weekend. Oh, you'll look so beautiful in a long, white dress!

Nancy: Mom, I'm not going to spend hundreds of dollars on a dress that I'll never wear again.

Nancy's mother: But your father and I will pay for it!

Nancy: No, Mother. I'm going to wear a simple dress.

Tim: And I'm going to wear a suit. No rented tuxedo for me!

Nancy's mother: Now, what about the reception? We're going to have a big party with music and dancing, aren't we?

Nancy: No, Mom. Tim and I want to have something more simple. Will you and Dad have the reception at your house?

Nancy's mother: Well, it *is* traditional for the bride's parents to pay for the reception. I'm sure it'll be OK with your father. I'll ask him tonight.

Nancy: Thanks, Mom!

Using the following predictions from fortune cookies, ask and answer a yes/no question about each, using *be going to* or *will*.

► **EXAMPLE:** You will meet an interesting stranger.
Will I meet him at school?
No, you won't. You'll meet him at a party.

1. You will take a trip before the end of next month.
2. You're going to meet someone special soon.
3. Someone will ask you to keep a secret.
4. You're going to receive some money.
5. You will live a long and happy life.

For each of the verbs in the following story, use *will* or *be going to*, as appropriate. Use *be going to* for actions that will happen soon, and use *will* for more formal situations that will not happen soon. In some sentences, either one is correct.

According to sociologists, some immigrant parents in North America find it difficult to let their children go away to college in another city, state, or province after they graduate from high school. It is customary in North America to send young people away to the best possible university. North Americans feel that by going away to college, their children **(1)** _____ learn to be independent and self-sufficient, two qualities that are important in North American culture.

These immigrant parents, however, are worried about their children's safety. They're afraid that something bad **(2)** _____ happen to their son or daughter and they **(3)** _____ (not) be able to protect them. Some parents don't think their children **(4)** _____ be successful on their own. They're afraid that the young people **(5)** _____ fail, that they **(6)** _____ (not) be able to deal with everything, such as studying, doing laundry, and taking care of themselves. College officials and students say that these immigrant parents are also worried that their sons and daughters **(7)** _____ forget their families and **(8)** _____ (not want) to return home.

Many young high school graduates, on the other hand, want to go away to college. Giselle Siu, a senior at Houston High School, said to her parents, "Look, I **(9)** _____ be 18 soon, and legally I **(10)** _____ be able to leave home, with or without your permission." Other students are more sensitive when they try to persuade their parents. Alex Iavnoski, another high school senior, who just received a letter of acceptance from the University of Iowa, told his parents, "I **(11)** _____ answer this letter right away, and I **(12)** _____ say yes. And with my scholarship, I **(13)** _____ save you money, too. Someday you **(14)** _____ be very proud of me." Still others don't even apply to colleges that are out of state. "My mom and dad are super strict. I know what they **(15)** _____ say, so I **(16)** _____ apply to the local community college," says Ramón Sierra.

(Based on "Leaving Home" by Ana Veciana-Suárez, *Miami Herald*, April 16, 1993.)

▶ **EXERCISE 4**   *(Focus 4, page 39)*

Complete the following sentences about your future. Use *be going to* for plans and intentions, and use *will* for predictions.

▶ **EXAMPLE:** As a parent, I'm never going to hit my children. _____

1. As a parent, _____

_____

2. After class today, _____

_____

3. My horoscope today says that _____

_____

4. After the end of this term/semester, _____

_____

5. Next weekend, _____

_____

6. After graduation, _____

_____

7. Maybe on my next birthday, _____

_____

8. Ten years from now, _____

_____

9. My fortune cookie says that _____

_____

10. On my next vacation, _____

▶ **EXERCISE 5**   *(Focus 5, page 41)*

Respond to the following comments from your boss. Use the words from the list plus the correct form of *will* or *be going to*.

be better next year	go in July
be on time from now on	help you
call her as soon as I can	not happen again
get it right away	not tell anyone

1. "Where is that memo that I asked you to write?"

_____

2. "You were late for work three times this week."

_____

3. "When do you plan to take your vacation this year?"

_____

4. "I need someone to assist me with this special project."

_____

5. "Can you please ask Alexis if she wants to join us?"

_____

6. "Please don't tell anyone about our meeting. It's top secret."

_____

7. "Your annual evaluation was not very good, you know."

_____

8. "You were not very careful—you made a lot of mistakes on that report."

_____

Complete the crossword puzzle on page 21. If you need help, ask a classmate or native speaker of English.

```
            M
            A
            D
  C A S S A N D R A
            M
            E
```

ACROSS

1. Madame C., a gypsy, is a _____ teller who reads your palm and sees the future in her crystal ball.

6. Nickname for Albert

7. All right

9. Air conditioning (abbreviation)

11. When I first met Madame C., she was very formal and said, "How do you _____?"

13. Madame C., where will I be living _____ twenty years?

14. Exclamation

15. Past tense of *see*

17. Madame C. says that my children will be as American as apple _____.

18. Madame C., when I win the lottery, will I save or _____ all the money?

19. Part of a bookcase or cabinet that holds things

20. Opposite of *always*

24. Sugar and honey taste _____.

27. What I call my father

28. When you are critically ill, the hospital puts you in the _____ (abbreviation)

29. Madame C. says that I need a little _____ and _____, or rest and relaxation.

30. Madame C., last night I dreamt that I was a ballerina wearing a __ tu.

31. Advertisement (abbreviation)

33. Either: _____ : : Neither: nor

34. Madame C. predicts that I will meet one famous woman and two famous _____ .

35. What I call my mother

37. Madame C., is my life going to be full of happiness or _____ ?

DOWN

1. Fourth note in the musical scale

2. Opposite of *young*

3. If you are not a citizen of this country, you are a _____ citizen.

4. The abbreviation for electrocardiogram is ___ ___ G.

5. Madame C.'s name

8. Madame C. will tell you the past, the present, and _____ (2 words).

10. Madame C. sees someone in her crystal ball at a graduation ceremony wearing a _____ and gown.

12. 2, 4, 6, and 8 are even numbers, and 1, 3, 5, and 7 are _____ numbers.

13. Possessive of *it*

14. Petroleum

16. You and I

17. Physical education (abbreviation)

21. Rabbits and elephants have big _____ s.

22. Venereal disease (abbreviation)

23. Madame C.'s crystal ball is not square—it's _____ .

24. Madame C. saw in her crystal ball that I did something bad. She said, "_____ on you!"

25. *Old MacDonald had a farm,* ___ ___, ___ ___ O.

26. Prefix relating to the natural environment

30. The British are famous for their afternoon _____ .

32. Two (Spanish)

34. Multiple sclerosis (abbreviation)

36. Mr. : man : : _____ : woman

EXERCISES FOR THE TOEFL® TEST

Units 1–3

Choose the *one* word or phrase that best completes each sentence.

1. _____ a job yet?
   - (A) Does he has
   - (B) Does he have
   - (C) Has he
   - (D) He has

2. Yes, Don _____ in construction; he is a carpenter.
   - (A) doesn't work
   - (B) is working
   - (C) isn't working
   - (D) work

3. All the carpenters on his crew _____ new houses.
   - (A) build
   - (B) builds
   - (C) is building
   - (D) will building

4. Don says, " _____ twice and saws once."
   - (A) Always a good carpenter measures
   - (B) A good carpenter hardly measures ever
   - (C) A good carpenter always measures
   - (D) A good carpenter measures hardly ever

5. This is the reason that Don _____ costly mistakes.
   - (A) always make
   - (B) doesn't make
   - (C) isn't making
   - (D) is always make

6. As soon as I finish doing this, I _____ visit a fortune teller.
   - (A) 'm going to
   - (B) going to
   - (C) will
   - (D) will to

7. I _____ married next month, and I want to see what the stars say about my future.
   - (A) am going get
   - (B) 'm going to get
   - (C) will get
   - (D) won't get

8. Madame Cassandra read my palm and said, "There _____ romance in your life."

    (A) are going to be   (C) will be

    (B) not going to be   (D) won't to be

9. According to the fortune teller's crystal ball, I _____ someone new and fall in love.

    (A) going to meet   (C) will be meeting

    (B) 'm going to meet   (D) will meets

10. My fiancé found out. Now I have to promise him that _____ see Madame Cassandra anymore.

    (A) I'm going to   (C) I will

    (B) I'm not going to   (D) I won't

11. It used to be that an employee automatically retired at age 65, but nowadays people

    _____ off retirement, sometimes indefinitely.

    (A) are putting   (C) puts

    (B) is putting   (D) will put

12. It _____ that some people do it because they feel they need to keep busy; work has always been the center of their lives.

    (A) is seeming   (C) seems

    (B) seem   (D) will seem

13. These people don't know what to do with all the time that they now _____ during retirement.

    (A) are having   (C) has

    (B) is having   (D) have

14. Most of them _____ hobbies, and they don't know how to spend all this leisure time.

    (A) don't have   (C) no have

    (B) haven't   (D) won't have

15. Other people continue working because of economic necessity—the government Social Security check _____ enough to live on.

    (A) is often   (C) often is

    (B) is seldom   (D) seldom is

Identify the *one* underlined word or phrase that must be changed for the sentence to be grammatically correct.

16. Most North American children <u>begin</u> to work at home, where they <u>are having</u> daily
                                 A   **B**

    and/or weekly responsibilities, such as <u>washing</u> the dishes and <u>feeding</u> the dog.
                                           C   **D**

17. Children <u>receive</u> a weekly allowance <u>often</u>, which <u>is</u> a small amount of money, like a
           A   **B**   **C**

    salary, in exchange <u>for</u> doing these household chores or jobs.
                 D

18. The children <u>are using</u> this money <u>to buy</u> candy, soda, and things that <u>they</u> <u>need</u> for
                A   **B**   **C**   **D**
school.

19. Others <u>often</u> <u>save</u> <u>their</u> allowance and <u>making</u> bigger purchases: computer games, a pet,
          A   **B**   **C**   **D**
a musical instrument, or extra activities at summer camp.

20. The purpose of the allowance <u>is</u> to teach children the value of money and to teach them
                              A
responsibility—when they <u>don't work</u> and do a good job, they <u>aren't</u> <u>receive</u> the money.
                     B   **C**   **D**

21. North Americans <u>often</u> <u>eat</u> out at fast-food restaurants because they <u>no</u> <u>have</u> time to
                 A **B**   **C** **D**
prepare food at home.

22. These restaurants <u>serve</u> almost anything from pizza to fried chicken to hamburgers;
                 A
some people <u>eat</u> inside, and others <u>stay</u> in their car and <u>buying</u> their food from the
           B   **C**   **D**
drive-through window.

23. Some Americans <u>hardly</u> <u>never</u> <u>eat</u> at home; they <u>depend on</u> these inexpensive restaurants
             A   **B** **C**   **D**
for their meals.

24. For example, <u>never</u> my brother <u>prepares</u> his own food at home—he <u>always</u> goes out to
              A   **B**   **C**
fast-food restaurants and <u>eats</u> hamburgers and French fries.
                    D

25. <u>Are</u> you <u>think</u> it <u>is</u> healthy <u>to eat</u> that salty, processed, fried food?
   A   **B**   **C**   **D**

26. Karen and Steve, a modern young couple, <u>hardly never</u> <u>do</u> anything without a plan—they
                                   A   **B**
<u>always</u> <u>talk</u> together about plans for their jobs, their home, and their family.
 C   **D**

27. Karen <u>is</u> expecting; next month she and Steve <u>are going to</u> have a baby. Their doctor <u>will</u>
      A   **B**   **C**
<u>say</u> that Karen <u>is having</u> a normal pregnancy.
 D

28. Karen and Steve <u>are knowing</u> what they<u>'re going to</u> name the baby. If it's a girl, they<u>'ll</u>
               A   **B**   **C**
name her Susan, and if it's a boy, they <u>will</u> name him Richard.
                            D

29. Karen <u>is following</u> all the doctor's instructions. She<u>'s reading</u> a lot of books about
      A   **B**

pregnancy and childbirth, and she <u>won't take</u> classes at the local hospital. When the time
                                                  C

comes, she<u>'ll be</u> ready.
          D

30. It's time! Karen <u>is going to</u> have her baby very soon. She <u>will need</u> <u>to go</u> to the hospital
                A   **B**   **C**

right now, but Steve <u>can't</u> find the car keys.
                   D

ASKING QUESTIONS

Yes/No, Wh-, Tag Questions, Choice Questions

▶ **EXERCISE 1** *(Focus 1, page 50)*

Complete the yes/no questions using the correct form of each word in parentheses, paying attention to the italicized words. Practice saying the questions with rising intonation. Then ask three of your classmates the questions. Write their names and responses on separate paper. The first item has been completed as an example.

Questions
1. (can, swim)   _____Can_____ you ____swim____ ?   Susan: Yes, I can   Anna: Yes, I can.   Yuki: No, I can't.
2. (study)   _____ you *usually* _____ on Saturday?
3. (live)   _____ your mother _____ in the United States *right now?*
4. (will, study)   _____ you _____ English next year?
5. (would, eat)   _____ you _____ meat?
6. (be)   _____ English a difficult language for you?
7. (work)   _____ you _____ *right now?*

Questions
8. (be)   _____ I taller than you?
9. (working)   _____ you _____ *last night?*
10. (be)   _____ mathematics your favorite subject in elementary school?
11. (take)   _____ you _____ a vacation *last summer?*
12. (sing)   _____ you sometimes _____ in the shower?

▶ **EXERCISE 2** *(Focus 1, page 50)*

This is a yes/no question game that works best with six to ten students. All students sit in a circle. One student begins by asking the student on his or her left a yes/no question in the past tense. That student answers the question and then asks the student to his or her left a yes/no question in the present tense. That student answers the question and then asks the student on his or her left a yes/no question in the future tense. The game continues around the circle (past-tense question, present-tense question, future-tense question).

▶ **EXERCISE 3** *(Focus 1, page 50)*

Rewrite the questions in Exercise 1 as statement form questions. Read each question out loud. If possible, tape-record yourself and listen to make sure you are using question intonation. The first question has been written for you as an example.

1. You can swim? _____

2. _____

3. _____

4. _____

5. _____

6. _____

7. _____

8. _____

9. _____

10. _____

11. _____

12. _____

▶ **EXERCISE 4**   *(Focus 2, page 52)*

Think of six things you would like to know about three of your classmates. On separate paper, make a chart similar to the one in Exercise 1, but write your own questions. Then ask your classmates the questions and write their answers on the chart.

Question	Name _____	Name _____	Name _____
1. _____ _____			
2. _____ _____			
3. _____ _____			
4. _____ _____			
5. _____ _____			
6. _____ _____			

Verdieu Lucas is interviewing for a job as the director of the computer lab. Based on Verdieu's answers, write the questions the interviewer asks Verdieu. The first one has been done for you as an example.

Interviewer: Which job are you applying for? _____
Verdieu: I'm applying for the lab director's position.

Interviewer: _____

_____

Verdieu: I think my strong points are that I know a lot about computers and that I get along well with other people. Here's a copy of my resume.

Interviewer: _____

_____

Verdieu: I'm looking for a full-time position. However, I'm willing to accept a part-time position to begin with.

Interviewer: _____
Verdieu: My native country is Haiti.

Interviewer: _____
Verdieu: I left my last job one month ago.

Interviewer: _____
Verdieu: I left that job because my family moved here from Boston.

Interviewer: _____
Verdieu: I know how to use both Macintosh computers and PCs.

Interviewer: _____
Verdieu: I will be available to work just about anytime; however, I prefer to work during the day.

Interviewer: _____
Verdieu: I have my own car, so getting to work isn't a problem.

Interviewer: _____
Verdieu: I can start working right away.

Interviewer: _____
Verdieu: I expect about fifteen dollars per hour.

Choose one of the following jobs and role-play a job interview with a partner.

waiter/waitress	hotel desk clerk	gas station attendant
accountant	teacher's aide	singer in a nightclub
medical receptionist	mail carrier	driver for a florist
taxi driver	carpenter	salesclerk in a department store

▶ **EXAMPLE:** *Why do you want to work at this restaurant?*
Where have you worked before?
When can you start working?

You know some things about Laura's brothers and sister, but you can never remember which family member is which. Read the list on this page and ask your partner "who" questions about Laura's brothers and sister. Your partner will respond with information from the next page. Take turns asking the questions.

▶ **EXAMPLE: A:** *Who is the tallest?*
B: *Ken is the tallest.*

tallest	youngest	married
oldest	like Chinese food	single
play basketball in high school (past)	have children	pilot
visit Korea last year	like sports	artistic
start college next year	middle child	sings

KEN	JOY	BILL
26 years old/6 feet 3 inches tall	24 years old/5 feet 8 inches tall	18 years old/6 feet tall
married with two children	single	single
played basketball in high school	loves to travel	collects insects
likes all kinds of sports	went to Korea last year	paints, draws, and sings
pilot	likes Chinese food	entering college next year

▶ **EXERCISE 8**   *(Focus 3, page 54)*

**Write two questions for each sentence using the underlined words for cues. The first one
has been done for you as an example.**

▶ **EXAMPLE:** Right now, Glenn <u>lives</u> with <u>his parents</u>.

1. <u>Who lives with his parents?</u>

2. <u>Whom does Glenn live with?</u>

   <u>In two months</u>, he <u>will start</u> at the university.

3. _____

4. _____

   <u>He</u> went <u>with his uncle</u> to look for an apartment.

5. _____

6. _____

<u>They</u> found a nice <u>apartment</u> near the university, but it was a little expensive.

7. _____

8. _____

<u>Glenn</u> needs a <u>roommate</u>.

9. _____

10. _____

<u>Glenn</u> called several <u>friends</u>.

11. _____

12. _____

<u>Sean</u> also needed a <u>roommate</u>.

13. _____

14. _____

<u>Glenn</u> will share his apartment with <u>Sean</u>.

15. _____

16. _____

▶ **EXERCISE 9** *(Focus 4, page 57)*

Work with a partner. Practice asking and answering the questions in Exercise 8. Ask the questions in Exercise 8 as though you were not sure what you heard.

▶ **EXERCISE 10** *(Focus 6, page 60)*

Complete the following dialogues by adding the tag questions and completing the responses. The first one has been done for you.

<u>**Dialogue 1**</u>

Catherine: You're taking a math class now, ___*aren't you*___?

Jim: Yes, _____.

Catherine: Diana is in your class, _____?

Jim: Yes, _____.

Catherine: You both have to study a lot for that calculus class, _____?

Jim: Yes, _____.

Catherine: You'll finish that class soon, _____?

Jim: Yes, _____.

Catherine: Only three more weeks! Great. You're going to take a vacation after that,

_____?

Jim: Yes, _____. I'm going to visit my family.

Catherine: Oh, I know you'll enjoy that.

Dialogue 2

Guillermo: You don't have any aspirin, _____? I have a giant headache.

Chris: No, sorry _____. You aren't getting sick, _____? You don't look so good.

Guillermo: No, I'm all right.

Chris: You didn't eat very much today, _____?

Guillermo: No, that's not the problem. I was working on the computer all day, and my eyes are tired.

Chris: Oh, that's the problem. You're right. You need some aspirin.

Guillermo: The pharmacy down the street is open until 10:00, _____?

Chris: Yes, I think _____. But I don't think you should go. Let me go buy something for your headache.

Guillermo: Okay. Let me get you some money. I think five dollars should be enough,

_____?

Chris: Sure. That's more than enough.

▶ **EXERCISE 11**   *(Focus 7, page 63)*

Read the dialogues in Exercise 10 with a partner. Read the first dialogue as though you are sure what your partner's answer will be. Read the second dialogue as though you are unsure. If possible, tape-record yourself and listen to see whether your intonation is rising or falling.

MODALS OF PROBABILITY AND POSSIBILITY

▶ **EXERCISE 1**   *(Focus 1, page 72)*

You have found a purse containing the following items. Write the best answer in each space to complete the statements about the owner of the purse. Be prepared to explain your answers.

1. a driver's license with a female photo and name

   The owner of the purse _____ a woman.
       (A) could be   (B) is   (C) may be

2. a comb with gray hairs

   She _____ an older woman.
       (A) could be   (B) might be   (C) must be

3. a government employee ID card

   She _____ for the government.
       (A) could work   (B) may work   (C) must work

4-5. a lot of keys and computer disks

   The _____ a secretary.
       (A) could be   (B) is   (C) must be

   She _____ a computer.
       (A) doesn't use   (B) must use   (C) uses

6. pictures of children

   The children _____ her grandchildren, or they _____ her nieces and nephews.
       (A) are   (B) could be   (C) might be

7. a glass case

She _____ wear glasses, but the case _____ be for sunglasses.

        (A) could   (B) may   (C) must

8. a bank statement showing a balance of $0.

She _____ any money in the bank, but she _____ another account.

       (A) could have   (B) doesn't have   (C) must have

9. an Irish passport full of stamps

She _____ be American. She _____ travel a lot.

       (A) might   (B) must   (C) must not

10. a small handgun

She _____ work for the police. She _____ be a spy.

       (A) could   (B) might   (C) must

▶ **EXERCISE 2**   *(Focus 2, page 74)*

Unscramble the following statements of probability/possibility about some classmates.

▶ **EXAMPLE:** Lee hasn't smiled all day.

        a / bad / be / he / in / mood / must <u>He must be in a bad mood.</u>

1. Every time I see Gigi, she's eating a candy bar.

   chocolate / like / must / she _____

2. Every day Julia wears a white dress with white stockings and shoes to class.

   a / be / might / nurse / she _____

3. Juan always carries a helmet.

   a / he / motorcycle / must / ride _____

4. Oleg and Natalya have the same last name and come to class together.

   be / must / related / they _____

5. Oleg is 19 years old, and Natalya is 27.

   be / couldn't / mother / Natalya / Oleg's _____

6. Is Lin's study group going to meet this week?
I don't know.

   because / is / Lin / not / might / sick / it _____

7. Jacques gets up in the middle of class and leaves the room.

   he / know / may / not / rude / that's _____

8. Nancy wears a diamond ring, and she's always talking about a man named Tim.

be / engaged / must / she _____

9. Claudia's family has a car, but Claudia walks to school or takes the bus.

drive / how / know / might / not / she / to _____

10. Who is that new student? I never saw her before.

be / class / could / in / she / the / wrong _____

Now, using *could, may, might,* **or** *must,* **write three statements of probability/possibility about your own classmates. Be ready to support each statement with specific observations.**

_____

_____

_____

▶ **EXERCISE 3** *(Focus 3, page 77)*

After reading the following dialogue, rewrite the phrases and sentences in bold type, using *could, may, might,* **or** *must.* **Be careful—some are in the present tense, and others are in the past tense. The first one has been done for you.**

Gladys and her husband Norman are talking about their neighbors. Gladys is convinced that they are terrible people, but Norman isn't so sure. He thinks that Gladys is being a nosy neighbor and jumping to conclusions.

Gladys: Have you seen the car the Riccios are driving? It's a Mercedes Benz! He's a handyman and she's a secretary. **It's not possible for them to make enough money to afford that car. They are probably drug dealers.**

1. They couldn't make enough money to afford that car. _____

2. _____

Norman: Oh, Gladys. Mind your own business. **Maybe they inherited the money, or it's possible that they won the car** in a contest. We don't know!

3. _____

4. _____

Gladys: And did you see their recycling container last week? **It looked like there were a dozen wine bottles. I think they are alcoholics.**

5. _____

6. _____

Norman: Oh, Gladys. Mind your own business. **It's possible that Kathy and Tim had a party, or maybe they invited friends over for dinner.**

7. _____

8. _____

Gladys: Oh yeah? Well, two weeks ago I saw their car parked in front of St. Jude's Church. **Kathy probably went to** one of those Alcoholics Anonymous meetings that they hold there.

9. _____

Norman: Gladys, you don't know that for sure. **Maybe she was** at a store near the church. Mind your own business.

10. _____

Gladys: Norman . . . Have you seen their little boy lately? He has cuts and bruises all over his body. **I think Tim got drunk** and hit him. That's child abuse.

11. _____

Norman: Gladys, **it's possible the boy fell off his bike.** You know how kids are. Mind your own business.

12. _____

Gladys: Norman . . .

Norman: Gladys, **I think you're crazy.** You haven't even met those people!

13. _____

Gladys: **Maybe you're right,** Norman.

14. _____

**Using the following information and pictures, complete each sentence with *could, may,
might,* or *must* in the progressive. Be careful—some of them are negative.**

Jonathan, a college student, arrives at his family's home to pay his family a
surprise visit. He's worried because no one is there. As he looks around the house,
he's guessing what his family members are doing and what they were doing right
before he arrived.

Present progressive: to make a guess or draw a conclusion about something in progress at the
time of speaking

1. Dad sometimes takes an afternoon nap.

He _____

_____

2. But Dad's shoes aren't by the front door. When he comes home, Dad
always takes off his shoes and leaves them by the front door.

He _____

_____

3. The grocery list is not on the refrigerator, where my sister always puts
it. She does the family's grocery shopping every week.

My sister _____

_____

4. But the family car and my sister's bicycle are in the garage.

My sister _____

_____

5. My family walks the dog every day. Sparky, the family pet, isn't here.
My mom, dad, sister, and brother aren't here. The car and bikes are in
the garage.

Everybody _____

_____

Past Progressive: to make a guess or draw a conclusion about something that was in progress before the time of speaking

6. My mom's coffee cup is half empty, and the coffee is still warm.

She _____

_____

7. The chess set is on the table—my sister and brother often play together.

They _____

_____

8. Dad's glasses and a book are next to his favorite chair.

He _____

_____

9. My sister's Rollerblades™ are by the door.

My sister _____

_____

10. There are a lot of cigarette butts in the ashtray, and the house smells awful.

Someone _____

_____

▶ **EXERCISE 5**   *(Focus 5, page 81)*

Choose the best answer and write it in the space.

1. A: What are you going to do this weekend?

B: My brother has tickets to the baseball game, so I _____ with him. My favorite team is playing.
(A) could go   (B) 'll probably go   (C) must go

2. A: What are you going to do on your vacation?

B: I'm not sure. We _____ a trip to Kenya and go on a safari.
(A) 'll probably take   (B) may take   (C) must take

3. A: Do you have plans for tonight?

   B: Not really. I _____ just stay home and watch TV, as usual.
   (A) could   (B) 'll probably   (C) must

4. A: I wonder why Mike is wearing that bandage around his wrist.

   B: I don't know. He _____ it.
   (A) might hurt   (B) must have hurt   (C) must hurt

5. A: Where are my keys?

   B: You _____ them in the kitchen.
   (A) may leave   (B) might have left   (C) must leave

6. A: I haven't been feeling well lately, especially in the morning.

   B: Really? You _____ pregnant. Maybe you've got morning sickness.
   (A) could be   (B) 'll probably be   (C) must be

7. A: Have you seen Lourdes?

   B: Yes, and judging from the size of her stomach, she _____ at least seven months pregnant.
   (A) could have been   (B) 'll probably be   (C) must be

8. A: Are you going to visit your family this year?

   B: I don't know. It depends on the airfares. I _____.
   (A) could be   (B) may be   (C) might

9. A: What grade do you think you'll get in this class?
   B: So far I have a pretty good average, and I've been studying a lot this semester.

   I _____ a B.
   (A) could get   (B) 'll probably get   (C) must get

10. A: Her hair always looks so stiff and thick.
   B: I know. It looks very unnatural.

   A: She _____ a wig.
   (A) 'll probably wear   (B) might wear   (C) must wear

UNIT 6

PAST PROGRESSIVE AND SIMPLE PAST WITH TIME CLAUSES

When, While, and As Soon As

▶ **EXERCISE 1** *(Focus 1, page 90)*

Imagine that you are the victim of the Gentleman Jewel Thief in the following cases. Use the pictures to explain each robbery to the police. Using the past progressive *(was/were talking)* or simple past *(talked)*, write your answers to the questions in each case. The first one has been done for you.

CASE #1

VERONICA RIO

1. Miss Rio, what were you doing at the time of the robbery?

I was having a drink at the Yacht Club.

2. Please describe the man who stole your jewels.

3. What did you do immediately after the thief stole your jewels?

_____

CASE #2

EVA GALOR

4. Mrs. Galor, where were you and what were you doing at the time of the crime?

_____

5. Could you give us a description of the thief?

_____

6. Did the thief have a mustache?

_____

7. What did you do immediately after the thief stole your jewels?

_____

CASE #3

RUTH ROX

8. Mrs. Rox, what were you ladies doing when the thief stole your jewels?

_____

9. What did the thief look like?

_____

10. What was he wearing?

_____

11. Did he speak with an accent?

_____

12. What did you all do after he took your jewels?

_____

▶ **EXERCISE 2**   *(Focus 2, page 91)*

Imagine that you were at the bank when a robbery occurred. Test your observation skills by studying the following picture for two minutes. Then, using the past progressive, write as many sentences as you can about what was happening at the time of the robbery.

1. _____

_____

2. _____

_____

3. _____

_____

4. _____

_____

5. _____

_____

6. _____

_____

7. _____

_____

8. _____

_____

9. _____

_____

10. _____

_____

▶ **EXERCISE 3**   *(Focus 2, page 91)*

Using the picture of the bank from Exercise 2, complete the following conversation between a detective and a bank teller. Use the past progressive or the simple past, depending on the question.

   1. Detective: Where was the manager at the time of the robbery? What was the manager doing?

       Teller: _____

_____

2. Detective: Was the security guard there? What was he doing?

Teller: _____

_____

3. Detective: Were there any other employees at the bank? What were they doing?

Teller: _____

_____

4. Detective: Were any customers standing in line? (If so, how many?)

Teller: _____

_____

5. Detective: Please describe the person who was first in line.

Teller: _____

_____

6. Detective: Please describe the person who was last in line.

Teller: _____

_____

7. Detective: Was anyone acting suspiciously? (*acting suspiciously:* appearing to be doing something wrong)

Teller: _____

_____

8. Detective: What time was it?

Teller: _____

_____

9. Detective: You said that there was a man outside the door. What was he wearing?

Teller: _____

_____

10. Detective: What were you doing at the time of the robbery? _____

Teller: _____

_____

Using the pictures from Exercise 1, indicate whether each of the following statements is true (T) or false (F). If the statement is false, rewrite it to make it true, using *when, while,* or *as soon as.*

T   F   **1.** Veronica Rio kissed the thief when he stole her jewels.

T   F   **2.** Ms. Rio had a drink as soon as the thief took her jewels.

T   F   **3.** While Veronica was having a drink, the Gentleman Jewel Thief began to talk to her.

T   F   **4.** While Eva Galor was shouting, the thief took her jewels.

T   F   **5.** The thief was wearing sunglasses and a hat when the second robbery took place. (*took place:* happened)

T   F   **6.** As soon as the thief took her jewels, Eva said, "Thank you."

T   F   **7.** Mrs. Rox and her friends were playing cards when the third crime took place.

T   F   **8.** As soon as the Gentleman Jewel Thief took their jewels, the women played bridge.

T   F   **9.** The thief was probably wearing a disguise when he committed these crimes. (*disguise:* something to change his appearance)

T   F   **10.** While the Gentleman Jewel Thief was committing his crimes, he was rude to his victims.

► EXERCISE 5   *(Focus 4, page 94)*

Rewrite all the sentences from Exercise 4, changing the order of the clauses and the punctuation. The first one is done for you.

1. When the thief stole her jewels, Veronica Rio ran after him.

2. _____

_____

3. _____

_____

4. _____

_____

5. _____

_____

6. _____

_____

7. _____

_____

8. _____

_____

9. _____

_____

10. _____

_____

EXERCISES FOR THE TOEFL® TEST

Units 4–6

Choose the *one* word or phrase that best completes each sentence.

1. Maureen needed some money yesterday to buy gas for her car, so she _____ to the bank.
   - (A) didn't go
   - (B) could have been going
   - (C) was going
   - (D) went

2. _____ Maureen was getting cash at an ATM, someone came up behind her and robbed her.
   - (A) After
   - (B) As soon as
   - (C) Before
   - (D) While

3. The thief _____ a T-shirt and blue jeans and had big tattoos all over his arms.
   - (A) was wearing
   - (B) weared
   - (C) may have worn
   - (D) might worn

4. He was holding something in his hand. Maureen thought that it _____ a gun.
   - (A) could be
   - (B) could been
   - (C) might have been
   - (D) was being

5. _____ she realized what happened, Maureen ran to a phone, called the police, and reported the crime.
   - (A) As soon as
   - (B) Before
   - (C) During
   - (D) While

6. The first question that the police asked her was, _____
   - (A) "You are okay, ma'am, are you?"
   - (B) "Would you be okay, ma'am?"
   - (C) "Are you okay, ma'am?"
   - (D) "You could be okay, ma'am, couldn't you?"

7. The second question that the police asked was, _____
   - (A) "What did happen?"
   - (B) "What's happening?"
   - (C) "What must have happened?"
   - (D) "What happened?"

8. Then they asked her, _____

  (A) "How much money could he take?"

  (B) "How much money did he take?"

  (C) "How much money was he taking?"

  (D) "How much money did he took?"

9. Maureen was lucky because her keys were still in her pocket. With her keys, the thief _____ her car.

  (A) could have stolen

  (B) must have stolen

  (C) was stealing

  (D) stole

10. But the thief stole her money and her credit cards. Without money, Maureen _____ buy gas, and she had to walk home.

  (A) could

  (B) couldn't

  (C) might

  (D) might not

11. Later, the police told Maureen that she hadn't been very careful. The thief was standing near the bank, and she _____ noticed him.

  (A) could

  (B) could have

  (C) must

  (D) must have

12. They also told her that she was very lucky. She _____ hurt very seriously.

  (A) could been

  (B) may be

  (C) might have been

  (D) must be

13. Two days later, someone _____ Maureen's purse, with all of her identification and credit cards, in a trash can.

  (A) may have found

  (B) found

  (C) was finding

  (D) was found

14. The police called Maureen and told her the good news. "You know, all in all, you are a very lucky lady, Ms. O'Hara, _____ ?

  (A) do you

  (B) don't you

  (C) are you

  (D) aren't you

Identify the *one* underlined word or phrase that must be changed for the sentence to be grammatically correct.

15. A 28-year-old woman <u>may become</u> the next princess. The prince <u>was making</u> his decision
          A   **B**
<u>after</u> he <u>consulted</u> his list of more than 100 candidates.
  C   **D**

16. At first she <u>didn't</u> want to be on the "princess list." People <u>said</u> that she <u>must</u> <u>had</u> a
                    A   **B**   **C**   **D**
boyfriend.

17. But the prince <u>started</u> calling her on the telephone every day. He <u>must have been</u> very
                      A   **B**
convincing, because as soon as he <u>was doing</u> this, she <u>changed</u> her mind.
                                    C   **D**

18. The future princess <u>is</u> a very independent and well-educated woman. Princesses in the
                        A

past <u>were</u> very traditional women. She <u>may</u> <u>changed</u> the very conservative role of
   B   **C**   **D**

princess.

19. <u>While</u> she <u>was living</u> in Australia, she <u>must have worked</u> as a diplomat. She speaks five
   A   **B**   **C**

languages and <u>studied</u> in four countries.
            D

20. <u>Why</u> do you think about the prince's choice? <u>Do</u> you think he <u>made</u> the right decision?
   A   **B**   **C**

<u>Do</u> you think the princess will be happy?
 D

SIMILARITIES AND DIFFERENCES

Comparatives, Superlatives, As . . . As, Not As . . . As

► EXERCISE 1   *(Focus 1, page 106)*

Psychologists doing research on the brain find that some people use the right side of their brain more than the left side. Other people depend more on the left side of the brain when they have to solve a problem or learn something. A third group of people have no clear preference; they use both sides of the brain equally. The chart below shows some of the different characteristics of "right-brain" and "left-brain" people. Using the information from the chart on page 52, complete the following sentences with the appropriate form of the comparative or superlative. The first one is done as an example.

LEFT-BRAIN PEOPLE

1. They are _____less_____ emotional _____than_____ right-brain people.

2. They speak _____ skillfully _____ right-brain people.

3. They shop _____ carefully _____ people in the right-brain category.

4. The _____ competitive individuals of all the groups are left-brain dominant.

5. They are _____, or more organized, _____ right-brain people.

6. They like to fix things _____ right-brain people do.

RIGHT-BRAIN PEOPLE

7. They are _____ artistic _____ left-brain people.

8. They probably have _____ friends _____ people in the other two categories.

Left-Brain	Right-Brain	Integrated
Logical, rational	Artistic, emotional	No clear preferences, flexible
Verbal—good speaking skills	Nonverbal	
Worry about details	Look at the whole picture	
Conservative	Liberal	
Want to be in control	Take risks*	
Neat, organized	Look unorganized but know where things are	
Always on time or early	Rarely on time	
Competitive	Cooperative	
Good at algebra	Good at geometry	
Make lists of day's activities	Picture (i.e., "see in their mind") places, people, things they have to do	
After meeting someone for the first time, they remember the person's name	After meeting someone for the first time, they remember the person's face	
When shopping, they buy after reading labels, comparing prices	When shopping, they buy on impulse	
When explaining a plan, they do it orally	When explaining a plan, they prefer to use paper and pencil	
Prefer to work alone	Outgoing and work well with others	
Enjoy sewing, chess	Enjoy skiing and/or swimming	
Enjoy doing crossword puzzles	Enjoy fishing and/or running	
Like to plan trips	Like surprises	
Like to fix things around the house	Like to rearrange furniture at home	

*a risk: a chance, danger of losing something important.

9. They are ＿＿＿＿＿＿ punctual ＿＿＿＿＿＿ left-brain people.

10. They are ＿＿＿＿＿＿ cooperative ＿＿＿＿＿＿ people in the first group.

11. They like surprises ＿＿＿＿＿＿ left-brain people do.

12. The ＿＿＿＿＿＿ outgoing people of all the groups are in this category.

Check (√) your personal preferences in the chart below. Count the total number of checkmarks you have in each category to decide whether you are left- or right-brain dominant. Compare your answers with your classmates' answers. Then, using the comparative and superlative forms, write sentences on the next page comparing yourself with the other members of the class.

LEFT	RIGHT	NO PREFERENCE
____ I'm logical and rational.	____ I'm artistic and emotional.	____
____ I'm verbal; I speak well.	____ I'm nonverbal.	____
____ I worry about details.	____ I look at the "whole picture."	____
____ I'm conservative.	____ I'm liberal.	____
____ I want to be in control.	____ I take risks.	____
____ I'm neat and organized.	____ I seem unorganized, but I know where things are.	____
____ I'm on time or early.	____ I'm rarely on time.	____
____ I'm competitive.	____ I'm cooperative.	____
____ I'm good at algebra.	____ I'm good at geometry.	____
____ I make lists of my day's activities.	____ I picture (i.e., "see in my mind") my day's activities.	____
____ After I meet someone for the first time, I remember the person's name.	____ After I meet someone for the first time, I remember the person's face.	____
____ When I'm shopping, I buy after reading labels and comparing prices.	____ When I'm shopping, I buy on impulse.	____
____ To explain a plan, I prefer to speak.	____ To explain a plan, I prefer to use a pencil and paper.	____
____ I prefer to work alone.	____ I'm outgoing and work well with others.	____
____ I enjoy sewing and/or chess.	____ I enjoy skiing and/or swimming.	____
____ I like doing crossword puzzles.	____ I like fishing and/or running.	____

___ I like to plan trips.

___ I like surprises.

___

___ I like to fix things around the house.

___ I like to rearrange the furniture at home.

___

___ **Total**

___ **Total**

___ **Total**

▶ EXAMPLE: <u>Susan is more artistic than I.</u>

<u>I take more risks than Susan and Mark.</u>

<u>Mark is the most competitive person in the group.</u>

1. _____
2. _____
3. _____
4. _____
5. _____
6. _____
7. _____
8. _____
9. _____
10. _____

Using the pictures and information below, complete the sentences with the comparative or superlative form of the word in parentheses.

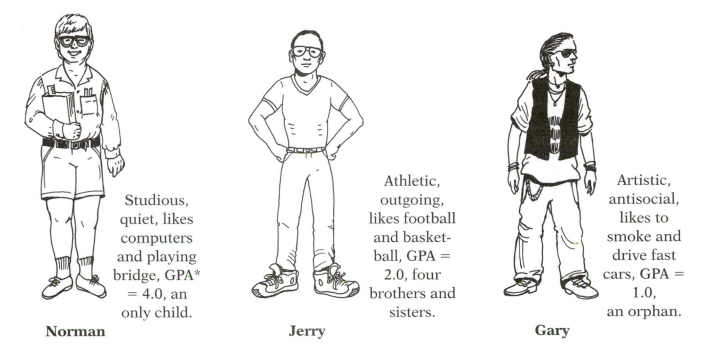

Studious, quiet, likes computers and playing bridge, GPA* = 4.0, an only child.

Norman

Athletic, outgoing, likes football and basket-ball, GPA = 2.0, four brothers and sisters.

Jerry

Artistic, antisocial, likes to smoke and drive fast cars, GPA = 1.0, an orphan.

Gary

*GPA: grade point average (on a 4-point scale, 4 is the highest grade and 0 is the lowest)

► **EXAMPLE:** As little boys, Gary and Norman were probably ___lonelier than___ Jerry. (lonely)

1. Of the three boys, Norman studies _____, and Gary studies _____. (hard)

2. Norman's hair is _____ Jerry's. (long)

3. Norman's glasses are _____ Jerry's. (thick)

4. Norman's belt is _____ the other boys' belts. (wide)

5. Of the three boys, Jerry has _____ feet. (big)

6. Of the three, Gary is wearing _____ pants. (tight)

7. Gary's hair is _____ Jerry's. (curly)

8. Norman and Jerry probably drive _____ Gary. (carefully)

9. Gary and Norman are probably _____ Jerry. (popular)

10. Jerry probably has _____ the other two boys. (friends)

Circle T if the statement is true and F if the statement is false. Use the information in the pictures from Exercise 3.

T F **1.** Jerry's GPA is almost as low as Gary's.

T F **2.** Norman is just about as handsome as Jerry.

T F **3.** Norman isn't as heavy as Gary.

T F **4.** Norman lives not nearly as dangerously as Gary.

T F **5.** Gary is practically as smart as Norman.

T F **6.** Norman is almost as tall as Gary.

T F **7.** Norman's pants are not as tight as Gary's.

T F **8.** Gary's hair is nowhere near as straight as Norman's.

T F **9.** Gary's grades are just about as bad as Jerry's.

T F **10.** Jerry's and Gary's grades are nearly as good as Norman's.

T F **11.** Norman plays football almost as well as Gary.

T F **12.** Gary's house is probably just as quiet as Norman's house.

Using the information from the chart in Exercise 1, complete the following sentences about Lois, a left-brain person, and Roy, a right-brain person. Use *less than*, *more than*, and *as . . . as*, and complete the sentence, if necessary.

▶ **EXAMPLE:** Roy's house is probably __not as clean as Lois's.__

1. Roy seems to be _____ organized _____ Lois.

2. Roy's closets probably aren't _____ neat _____ Lois's.

3. Lois doesn't take _____ risks as Roy _____.

4. Roy isn't _____ good at remembering names _____ Lois.

5. Of all her friends, Lois is _____ mechanical and _____ artistic.

6. Roy isn't _____ conservative _____ most of his friends.

7. Lois doesn't have _____ friends _____ Roy.

8. Lois probably doesn't like fishing _____ much _____ Roy _____.

9. Roy doesn't talk _____ much _____ Lois _____.

10. Roy likes decorating his house _____ Lois _____.

You are a teacher and you have to talk to the parents of one of your students. In each of the following pairs, put a checkmark next to the polite and less direct way to compare their son Johnny with his classmates.

1. ___ Mr. and Mrs. Callahan, Johnny is not doing as well as the other students.

   ___ Mr. and Mrs. Callahan, Johnny is doing much worse than the other students.

2. ___ Johnny doesn't seem to study as much as the other boys and girls.

   ___ Johnny seems to study much less than the other boys and girls.

3. ___ Johnny's classmates concentrate more than he does in class.

   ___ Johnny doesn't concentrate as much as his classmates.

4. ___ The other students' spelling isn't as bad as Johnny's.

   ___ Johnny's spelling isn't as good as the other students'.

5. ___ When learning new lessons, the other boys and girls aren't as slow as Johnny.

   ___ When learning new lessons, Johnny isn't as fast as the other boys and girls.

6. ___ Johnny is less cooperative than his classmates.

   ___ Johnny isn't quite as cooperative as his classmates.

7. ___ The other boys and girls don't read as slowly as Johnny.

   ___ Johnny doesn't read as fast as the other boys and girls.

8. ___ The other students aren't as impolite as Johnny.

   ___ Johnny isn't as polite as the other students.

9. ___ In music class, the other boys and girls sing better than Johnny.

   ___ In music class, Johnny doesn't sing as well as the other boys and girls.

10. ___ All in all, Johnny is the worst student in the class.

   ___ All in all, Johnny isn't doing quite as well as his classmates.

MEASURE WORDS AND QUANTIFIERS

► **EXERCISE 1** *(Focus 1, page 122)*

Mrs. Griffin sent her husband shopping, but he ripped the shopping list. Can you help Mr. Griffin by completing the list? The first one has been done for you.

Grocery List

1. a bunch of bananas
2. _____ of bread
3. _____ eggs
4. _____ of lettuce
5. _____ of mayonnaise
6. _____ of dog food
7. _____ of cereal
8. _____ of radishes
9. _____ of white wine
10. _____ of ice cream

I went next door to borrow . . .

This is a game to test your memory. All players should sit in a circle. The first player begins by saying, "I went next door to borrow a can of anchovies" (or a bag of apples—any food that begins with the letter "A"). The second player repeats what the first player says and then adds another item, which begins with the letter "B." "I went next door to borrow a can of anchovies and a loaf of bread." The third player must repeat what the first two players have said and add another item, which begins with "C." "I went next door to borrow a can of anchovies, a loaf of bread, and a piece of cake," and so on until the whole alphabet has been completed.

Look at the grocery list in Exercise 1. Some of the items are count nouns (bananas) and some are noncount (bread). Write "C" beside each count noun and "NC" beside each noncount noun.

Using the food and measure words as cues, write the correct measure phrases to complete the following recipes. The first one has been done for you as an example.

AVOCADO ICE CREAM

2 ____cups of milk____ (milk, cup)

1/2 _____ (granulated sugar, cup)

1/4 _____ (salt, teaspoon)

2 _____ (egg)

1 _____ (heavy cream, cup)

2 _____ (lemon extract, teaspoon)

1 _____ (mashed avocado, cup)

- Combine milk, sugar, and salt; scald. Pour over eggs, stirring constantly. Add cream and lemon extract and cool.
- Add avocado and mix thoroughly. Freeze in ice-cream freezer. Makes about 1 quart.

CHEESE ENCHILADAS

1 _____ (corn tortillas, dozen)

1 _____ (enchilada sauce, heated, pint)

1 _____ (chopped onion, tablespoon)

1 _____ (shredded cheddar cheese, pound)

8 _____ (sour cream, ounce)

- For each enchilada, dip a tortilla into the enchilada sauce.
- Put some onion, cheese, and sour cream on the tortilla and roll the tortilla up.
- Pour the remaining sauce and sprinkle any leftover cheese on top. Bake at 325° for 30 minutes.

▶ **EXERCISE 5**   *(Focus 3, page 129)*

Look at the series of pictures below. Write a sentence describing each picture using a common quantifier. The first one has been done for you as an example. (Remember, *juice*, a noncount noun; *children*, a count noun.)

1.

2.

3.

4.

5.

6.

7.

8.

1. <u>There is no juice in the glass.</u>

2. _____

3. _____

4. _____

5. _____

6. _____

7. _____

8. _____

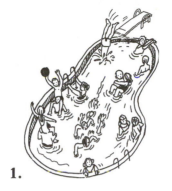

1.

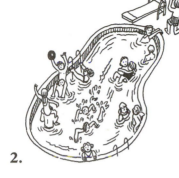

2.

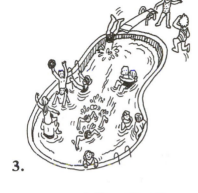

3.

4.

5.

6.

1. All of the children _____ are in the swimming pool. _____

2. _____ are in the swimming pool. _____

3. _____ are diving into the pool. _____

4. There are _____ in the pool. _____

5. _____ are lying next to the pool. _____

6. _____ are out of the pool.

7.   **8.**   **9.**

7. There are _____ in the pool.

8. There are _____ in the pool.

9. There are _____ in the pool.

UNIT 9

DEGREE COMPLEMENTS

Too, Enough, and Very

▶ **EXERCISE 1**   *(Focus 1, page 138)*

The Ganter family have just moved to Nashville. They have three young children, and they are looking for a house, but they don't think that they have enough money to buy a new house. The following is a list of characteristics they are looking for in a house that they gave their realtor:

- about $100,000
- older house
- four bedrooms
- two bathrooms
- large yard
- good school district

Their realtor gave them descriptions of the following houses. What do you think the Ganters said about each house? Write *enough, not enough,* or *too,* as appropriate, in each blank.

▶ **EXAMPLE:** There are ___*not enough*___ bathrooms.

1. The house is _____ modern.

2. There are _____ bedrooms.

3. The yard is _____ large _____.

4. The house is not _____ expensive.

Modern, beautiful home with all the conveniences: deluxe dishwasher, washer, dryer, side-by-side refrigerator and freezer. Three bedrooms, one bath. Small lot. $100,000.

5. There are _____ bedrooms.

6. There are _____ bathrooms.

7. The yard is large _____.

8. The house is cheap _____.

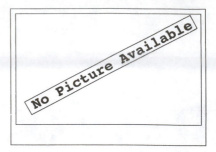

Built in 1926, this fixer-upper is loaded with space! Large lot. Four large bedrooms, two bathrooms. Old-fashioned breakfast room and pantry off the kitchen. $75,000.

9. The house is large _____.

10. There are _____ bathrooms.

11. The yard is _____ small.

12. The street is _____ busy for kids.

13. The house is _____ expensive.

Spacious four-bedroom, two baths, city house is right in the center of action right on the boulevard. Small yard easy to maintain with a pool. $125,000.

Penelope Picky is having an elegant party this weekend. She's spending all day preparing for the party, but she's very hard to satisfy. Fill in the blanks with *too, enough,* or *not enough,* as necessary. The following word list may help you, but don't limit yourself to those words. There are different ways to make meaningful responses for this exercise. Compare your answers with a partner's.

softly	loudly	large
rich	fattening	cold
elegantly	wildly	short
long	seriously	silly
light	sophisticated	sexy
quietly	weird	tight
loose	stylish	sweet
musicians	dessert	calories
toppings	spots	time
space	money	

AT THE CATERER'S

► **EXAMPLE:**   **Caterer:** *What would you like to serve for dessert, madam? Cheesecake?*

Penelope: No, cheesecake is too fattening, and you never serve enough.

1.   **Caterer:** Ice cream?

Penelope: No, _____.

2.   **Caterer:** Chocolate mousse?

Penelope: No, _____.

3.   **Caterer:** Pastries?

Penelope: No, _____.

   Caterer: Flan?

Penelope: Yes, that would be perfect. It's not too sweet, and it will be elegant enough.

AT THE DEPARTMENT STORE BUYING
A DRESS FOR THE PARTY

4. Salesclerk: What about this miniskirt?

   Penelope: No, _____.

5. Salesclerk: Perhaps you would prefer this elegant long dress?

   Penelope: No, _____.

6. Salesclerk: What about this leopard skin print?

   Penelope: Definitely not, _____.

7. Salesclerk: How about this one?

   Penelope: Yes, _____.

AUDITIONING MUSICIANS FOR THE PARTY

8.   Agent: What about a rock band?

   Penelope: No, _____.

9. **Agent:** A string quartet?

Penelope: No, _____.

10. **Agent:** I know a great country and western band.

Penelope: No, _____.

11. **Agent:** What about a jazz quartet?

Penelope: Perfect, _____.

▶ **EXERCISE 3** *(Focus 3, page 142)*

Complete the following story by filling in each blank with *too much, too many, too little,* or *too few,* as appropriate.

Robin Bird: Good evening, folks. This is Robin Bird with another fascinating episode of *Lifestyles of the Extremely Rich.* We're here today with Ms. Mercedes Benz at her fabulous home, San Coupe, in California. Thanks for having us.

Mercedes: Certainly, Robin.

Robin: Mercedes, do you really have 12 bathrooms here at San Coupe?

Mercedes: Well, yes, Robin. I do have 12 bathrooms. Do you think that's **(1)** _____ bathrooms?

Robin: No, of course not. But it must take quite a few servants to keep all those bathrooms clean.

Mercedes: You're right, I never have enough servants. There are always **(2)** _____ servants around, and it takes **(3)** _____ energy to manage all of them, but I get by somehow.

Robin: Let's talk about the grounds surrounding San Coupe. How much land do you own?

Mercedes: Well, I'm just not sure how much land I own, but I know I have **(4)** _____ grass to mow in one day, and I have three swimming pools. Unfortunately, I don't get enough exercise because I just bought two new cars, and now I have **(5)** _____ time to do much swimming.

Robin: How many cars do you own now?

Mercedes: Seven, one for each day of the week. Of course, now I have the problem of **(6)** _____ garage space. But that's what happens when you have **(7)** _____ cars.

Robin: Can you believe that, folks? Seven cars! Well, we have to go, but Mercedes, I want to thank you very much for sharing San Coupe with us. I hope we didn't take up

(8) _____ of your time.

Mercedes: It was my pleasure, Robin. A woman like me can never get (9) _____

publicity. I get (10) _____ opportunities to show off San Coupe.

▶ **EXERCISE 4**   *(Focus 4, page 143)*

List things you like and don't like about where you live now. Use *too* and *very* in your description. Then share your list with a partner.

▶ EXAMPLE: My apartment has *too* few rooms.

My living room is *very* sunny.

THINGS I LIKE

_____

_____

_____

THINGS I DON'T LIKE

_____

_____

_____

Exercises for the TOEFL® Test

Units 7–9

Choose the *one* word or phrase that best completes each sentence.

1. Thai food is hotter than Japanese food; by *hotter*, I mean _____ .
    (A) as spicy
    (C) spicier
    (B) less spicy
    (D) a little spicy

2. It's _____ for people who don't like spicy food.
    (A) as hot
    (C) hotter
    (B) hot enough
    (D) too hot

3. It can be spicy hot like Indian food, but _____ as Indian food.
    (A) as greasy
    (C) more greasy
    (B) less greasy
    (D) not as greasy

4. Thai cuisine is _____ and more exotic than heavy French food.
    (A) as light
    (C) lighter
    (B) less light
    (D) more light

5. Like the French chefs, Thai cooks use _____ fresh herbs and spices.
    (A) enough
    (C) too few
    (B) many
    (D) too many

6. *Satay* is one of my favorite Thai dishes. It consists of meat served with a wonderful

peanut sauce. You can make the sauce at home or buy _____ of it at a gourmet shop.
    (A) a clove
    (C) a box
    (B) a bottle
    (D) a scoop

7. *Satay* was originally Indonesian, but the Indonesian dish isn't _____ as the *satay* from Thailand.
    (A) as spicy
    (C) quite spicy
    (B) less spicy
    (D) spicier

8–9. In my opinion, of _____ the world's cuisines, Asian cooking is _____ .

    (A) a couple of   (A) delicious

    (B) none of   (B) more delicious

    (C) all   (C) most delicious

    (D) few   (D) the most delicious

10. Roy had a heart attack last year. Before that, he had never worried _____ about his health. His doctor told him to change his lifestyle and gave him a diet and exercise plan.

    (A) too little   (C) very much

    (B) enough   (D) a great deal of

11. To have a more healthful diet, Roy started to eat _____ fruits and vegetables and _____ fat.

    (A) fewer . . . less   (C) some . . . much

    (B) more . . . more   (D) more . . . less

12–13. Instead of eating a _____ of chocolate when he wanted something sweet, Roy learned to eat an apple or a _____ of grapes.

    (A) box   (A) bunch

    (B) bar   (B) dozen

    (C) clove   (C) leaf

    (D) tablet   (D) scoop

14–15. Before his heart attack, he ate _____ fast food, and he almost never ate _____ fresh fruits and vegetables.

    (A) many   (A) more

    (B) a lot of   (B) very much

    (C) enough   (C) a few

    (D) too little   (D) very many

Identify the *one* underlined word or phrase that must be changed for the sentence to be grammatically correct.

16. Before his heart attack, Roy's diet wasn't as healthy as it is now. He ate alot of salty and
                                        A   **B**   **C**
fried food, and he didn't eat very much healthy food.
                         D

17. He still eats dessert, but now he has a bowl of frozen yogurt instead of a few scoops of ice
                              A   **B**   **C**
cream. Frozen yogurt doesn't have as much fat than ice cream.
                               D

18. Roy has a much better lifestyle now. In addition to a healthyer diet, he's getting more
               A   **B**   **C**
exercise, and he's smoking a lot less.
                D

19. It's been one year since Roy had his heart attack, and he feels much better than he did
                                                                                              A   **B**
before. He quit smoking, lost too much weight, and continues to exercise a lot.
                                              C   **D**

20. Roy's family is very happy—they love him too much and are glad that he's taking better
                                    A   **B**   **C**
care of himself than he did before his heart attack.
        D

21. Roy's also not under as much stress as before; he quit his job because it was too stressful
                                  A   **B**
for him, and he's a lot more happier now.
  C   **D**

22. His doctor says that if he continues to do as well as he's doing now, the risk of having
                                                                        A
another heart attack will be much less, and Roy will live a lot more long.
                          B   **C**   **D**

23. I think North American food is less interesting than other cuisines; it's one of the
                                      A   **B**
blander, least imaginative cuisines that I know.
  C   **D**

24. It uses too little spices and fresh herbs and too many canned and frozen ingredients.
                    A   **B**   **C**   **D**

25. Other cooks around the world use a much wider variety of herbs and spices, so their food
                                                A   **B**
has more flavor than we do.
        C   **D**

26. North Americans eat a lot of processed and frozen foods, which have chemicals and are
not as healthful than diets with more fresh, natural foods.
  A   **B**   **C**   **D**

27. They also eat at fast-food restaurants, which serve greasy food with a lot of calories.
                                                                                                A
That's part of the reason that North Americans are much fatter and less healthy that
                                                                B   **C**   **D**
people of other nationalities.

28. Not all North Americans eat fast food; some enjoy trying international food very much,
  A   **B**
but preparing that food at home isn't enough convenient for them.
                                                C   **D**

29. Yes, some have started to change their attitudes towards food, but no enough—the
    A   **B**
average North American still eats too many mashed potatoes and too much Hamburger
                              C   **D**
Helper.

30. If North Americans borrowed more ideas from the cuisines of their various ethnic
                                        A
communities, they could learn a great deal and have some of a most fascinating cooking
                                        B   **C** **D**
in the world.

GIVING ADVICE AND EXPRESSING OPINIONS

Should, Ought To, Need To, Must, Had Better, Could, and Might

► **EXERCISE 1**   *(Focus 1, page 152)*

Advice columns appear in most North American newspapers. Readers write and ask for advice about their problems. Write four sentences of advice to the following people who are having problems. Use *should, should not,* or *ought to.* The first sentence has been done for you as an example.

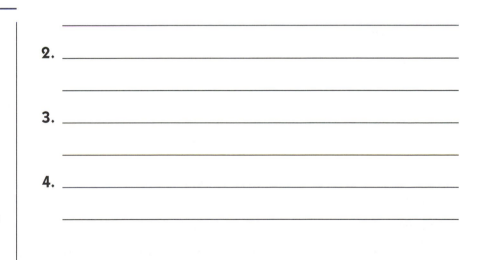

ASK GABBY

Dear Gabby,
I moved to Canada from Korea three years ago. My mom says I am forgetting my Korean heritage and I'm acting too much like a Canadian because I like playing hockey with my friends. I'm not trying to be disrespectful to my mom. I just want to be like the other kids. What should I do?

      Sincerely,
      On Thin Ice

1. First, you ought to talk to your mother.

2. _____

3. _____

4. _____

Dear Gabby,

I work all day as a cashier in a department store. When I come home, my husband expects me to make his dinner and clean the house. Not only that, but my husband is a slob. When he comes home from work, he leaves his clothes all over and then just watches TV. What should I do?

  Sincerely,
  Worn Out in
  Waukegan

1. _____

2. _____

3. _____

4. _____

Dear Gabby,

I'm a 25-year-old construction worker. I am very dissatisfied with my job. I've always wanted to help people. I'd like to study nursing, but all my friends say nursing is women's work. What should I do?

  Sincerely,
  Dissatisfied in Dallas

1. _____

2. _____

3. _____

4. _____

▶ **EXERCISE 2**   *(Focus 2, page 153)*

For each of the following situations, use the modal verbs in parentheses to give advice to the person with the problem.

▶ **EXAMPLE:** Lori lost her credit cards.

  (need to) *She needs to call the company and report that they are missing.*

  (should) *She should be more careful.*

Matthew plays the guitar. He wants to be a rock musician.

(ought to) **1.** _____

(shouldn't) **2.** _____

Bill got a speeding ticket.

(need to) **3.** _____

(should) **4.** _____

Kristi lost the necklace her boyfriend gave her.

(ought to) **5.** _____

(doesn't need to) **6.** _____

Geraldine forgot where she put her car keys.

(need to) **7.** _____

(should) **8.** _____

David's water pipes broke. There is water all over the kitchen.

(need to) **9.** _____

(shouldn't) **10.** _____

▶ **EXERCISE 3**   *(Focus 3, page 154)*

Complete the following sentences about Rosario, using *should, shouldn't, must,* or *must not,* as appropriate. Compare your answers with a partner. Explain why the answers you chose are most appropriate.

Rosario wants to be a doctor.

▶ **EXAMPLE:** She _____*should*_____ find out about medical schools.

   1. She _____ get high grades in college.

   2. She _____ like biology.

   3. She _____ study for seven years.

   4. She _____ find some friends who also want to be doctors so they can support each other and study together.

   5. She _____ apply for a scholarship.

   6. She _____ be afraid of blood.

   7. She _____ like to help people.

   8. She _____ be able to work long hours.

   9. She _____ work well under pressure.

   10. She _____ smoke cigarettes while examining patients.

Complete the following sentences with *should, ought to, had better,* or their negative forms.

▶ **EXAMPLE:** Mother to daughter: "You ___had better___ wear a warm jacket, or you'll catch cold."

1. At a train station: "You _____ buy your ticket. The train will be here in five minutes."

2. Parent to child: "You _____ eat your vegetables, or you won't get any dessert."

3. Teacher to student: "You _____ worry about this test. You'll do fine if you study. You got an A on all your other tests."

4. One student to another: "I agree we _____ study, but I'm ready for a break."

5. Boss to worker: "You _____ be late to work any more. If you come late again, you'll lose your job."

6. Worker to coworker: "Quick, we _____ look busy; the boss is coming."

7. Worker to coworker: "You _____ wear a tie to work if you want to impress the boss."

8. Travel agent to tourist: "You _____ leave home early, or you'll miss your flight because there is a lot of traffic at that time."

9. At the airport: "You _____ visit the pyramids while you are in Egypt. It's the chance of a lifetime!"

10. Police officer to driver: "You _____ not drive so fast, or you will get another speeding ticket."

For each of the following pairs, write a sentence using *should, ought to, had better,* or their negative forms.

1. Father to son: _____

   _____

2. Student to teacher: _____

   _____

3. Doctor to patient: _____

   _____

4. Mechanic to car owner: _____

   _____

It is the week before final exams, and Victoria and Migalie are trying to decide what they are going to do today. Complete the following dialogue using *should*, *could*, or *might*, as appropriate. The first one has been done for you as an example.

Victoria: We _____should_____ study for the biology exam.

Migalie: I know we _____, but it's such a beautiful day. Why don't we go to the beach? We _____ invite those cute guys who live in the next dorm.

Victoria: Sure, and we _____ go swimming.

Migalie: Yeah, we _____ play volleyball and get a great tan.

Victoria: I know—we _____ get some hamburgers and have a barbecue!

Migalie: But if we go to the beach, I _____ buy a new bathing suit because mine is getting old.

Victoria: Okay, you get a new bathing suit, and I'll get the food.

Migalie: Well, if we're going to invite those guys, you _____ get some burgers.

Victoria: You're right. We also _____ buy some picnic supplies.

Migalie: Wait, do you have any money?

Victoria: I _____ not. Let me look.

Migalie: I _____ not have enough, either.

Victoria: So, what _____ we do?

Migalie: We _____ study for the biology exam.

For each of the following situations, use *might, could, should, ought to, need to, had better, must,* or their negative forms to give advice. There are many possible answers to each situation. Explain why you chose the modal verb for a situation. After you have completed the exercise, compare answers with a partner.

HISHAM IS GETTING A DRIVER'S LICENSE.

▶ **EXAMPLE:** have an accident

He had better not have an accident while taking the road test.

Explanation: If he has an accident while taking the road test, he will not get his driver's license. A strong modal verb is necessary.

1. bring a passport or birth certificate _____

_____

Explanation: _____

_____

2. fail the written test _____

_____

Explanation: _____

_____

3. be nervous _____

_____

Explanation: _____

_____

4. practice parallel parking _____

_____

Explanation: _____

_____

ANGELICA IS REGISTERING FOR COLLEGE CLASSES.

5. get her advisor's signature _____

_____

Explanation: _____

_____

6. register early _____

_____

Explanation: _____

_____

7. find out about the instructors _____

_____

Explanation: _____

_____

8. buy her books before classes start _____

_____

Explanation: _____

_____

IT'S MY MOTHER'S BIRTHDAY.

9. buy her a card and gift _____

_____

Explanation: _____

_____

10. bake a cake _____

_____

Explanation: _____

_____

11. remind my father _____

_____

Explanation: _____

_____

BEN AND SARAH ARE WRITING RESEARCH PAPERS.

12. start researching early _____

_____

Explanation: _____

_____

13. turn in the paper late _____

_____

Explanation: _____

_____

14. type the paper _____

_____

Explanation: _____

_____

15. go to the library _____

_____

Explanation: _____

_____

DIEGO IS GETTING SICK.

16. call the doctor _____

_____

Explanation: _____

_____

17. go to bed _____

_____

Explanation: _____

_____

18. take some aspirin _____

_____

Explanation: _____

_____

▶ **EXERCISE 7** *(Focus 7, page 161)*

Do you agree or disagree with the following statements? Check (√) the appropriate column.

	Agree	Disagree
1. Men should help with the housework.	___	___
2. Women should not work outside the home.	___	___
3. Women should not be totally responsible for the child care.	___	___
4. Husbands ought to help their wives with the dishes.	___	___
5. Men and women should keep their traditional roles.	___	___
6. Boys shouldn't learn how to cook.	___	___
7. A college education ought to be available for both men and women.	___	___
8. Women should be encouraged to participate in athletics.	___	___
9. Wives ought to serve their husbands before they eat their own food.	___	___
10. A father should not help change the baby's diapers.	___	___
11. Women should learn how to change a tire.	___	___

▶ **EXERCISE 8** *(Focus 7, page 161)*

Compare your answers from Exercise 7 with your classmates'. Discuss your opinions.

Use *should, **ought to,*** or their negative forms and the cues below to express your opinions. Then compare your opinions with a partner.

► **EXAMPLE:** Men/help take care of children

<u>Men ought to help take care of children.</u>

1. Women with small children/work outside the home

_____

_____

2. Men/wash clothes

_____

_____

3. Boys/learn how to sew

_____

_____

4. Girls/learn how to repair cars

_____

_____

5. Boys and girls/go to school together

_____

_____

6. Women/participate in the Olympic Games

_____

_____

7. Women/become doctors

_____

_____

8. Teenagers/be able to drink alcohol

_____

_____

9. Students/study all the time

_____

_____

UNIT 11

MODALS OF NECESSITY AND PROHIBITION

Have To, Have Got To, Do Not Have To, Must/Must Not; Cannot

▶ **EXERCISE 1**   *(Focus 1, page 168)*

Put a check mark (√) by the sentences that are true.

1. ____ Before leaving on a trip abroad (to another country), you should get a travel book with information about that country.

2. ____ You shouldn't carry all of your money in cash, and you shouldn't put all your money in one place.

3. ____ To enter some tropical countries, you mustn't have some vaccinations and other shots to protect against tropical diseases.

4. ____ When you check in at the airport, you don't have to pay extra if you have too much luggage.

5. ____ You've got to pack your camera and passport in your suitcase.

6. ____ During the flight, you mustn't smoke in the nonsmoking section.

7. ____ When traveling abroad, you must learn to say *please* and *thank you* in the local language.

8. ____ To drive in North America, you have to have a driver's license.

9. ____ You should be able to carry all of your luggage by yourself.

10. ____ When you're in a North American city, you mustn't ask about neighborhoods that you should avoid (not go near).

11. ____ If you're lost in North America and you see a police officer, you should ask him/her for help.

Complete the following conversation by filling in each blank with the correct form of *must* **or** *have to,* **as indicated. When not indicated, answer with the pronoun and the auxiliary** *do.* **The first one has been done for you.**

Claudia and Andres, two foreign tourists, are renting a car. They're asking the agent about driving in the United States.

Andres: **(1)** __Do I have to__ (I + have to) have a driver's license?

Agent: Yes, **(2)** _____.

Andres: What about Claudia? She has an international driver's license. **(3)** _____ (she + have to) get another license?

Agent: No, **(4)** _____. She can drive here with an international license.

Claudia: What about seat belts? **(5)** _____ (we + have to) wear seat belts?

Agent: Yes, you **(6)** _____ (must) wear seat belts. It's the law in most states.

Andres: What **(7)** _____ (we + have to) do with that thing in the front seat of the car?

Agent: What thing? *(Andres points to the litter basket.)* Oh, that's the litter basket. It's for litter: garbage, paper, and things that you want to throw away.

Claudia: Can't we just throw those things out the window?

Agent: No, you **(8)** _____ (must + negative) throw anything out the window.

There's a $500 fine for littering! You **(9)** _____ (have to) keep everything inside the car.

Andres: **(10)** _____ (we + have to) drive on the left side of the road the way they do in England?

Agent: No! You **(11)** _____ (must + negative) drive on the left. Stay on the right.

Claudia: Are there any other laws that we should know about?

Agent: Well, if you're going to turn right or left, you **(12)** _____ (have to) use your

turn signal. On the highway, you **(13)** _____ (must) follow the speed limit,

and if you're driving more slowly than the other cars, you **(14)** _____ (have to) stay in the right lane. The left lane is for faster traffic. Obey the laws, or the police will stop you.

Fill in the blanks below with the correct form of *have to*. The first one has been done for you.

1. It's time for my yearly checkup. I ___have to___ remember to call the doctor's office sometime this month.

2. I burned my finger while I was cooking. The first-aid book says that I _____ hold my finger under cold water.

3. She spilled hot oil all over her leg and foot. John, You _____ take her to the emergency room now!

4. What _____ (Irene) do for her first-aid class? She _____ practice CPR (cardiopulmonary resuscitation).

5. His face is blue! We _____ check his throat to see what he's choking on.

6. There are jellyfish in the area. The lifeguard's telling Tommy that he _____ stay out of the water today.

7. Did that little girl drown? She stopped breathing. The lifeguard _____ start mouth-to-mouth respiration as soon as possible.

8. I cut my finger, and it's bleeding a little. What should I do?

   The neighbor, who's a nurse, says that you _____ wash the cut and then put a bandage on it.

9. There's something in my eye again!

   Oh, Lee. You _____ stop wearing so much eye makeup.

10. The children _____ get their vaccinations before school starts.

Some children are at a swimming pool with their grandmother. The lifeguard is shouting at the children, but they're not paying any attention. Their grandmother is repeating the lifeguard's instructions. In the spaces below, write what she says, using *cannot (can't)* **or** *must not (mustn't)*. **The first one is done for you.**

DIVING

1. Walk! No running!

   You mustn't run! or You must not run!

2. No diving in the shallow* water.

   _____

3. You're not allowed to go in the deep water until you pass a swimming test.

   _____

4. Don't take beach balls in the water.

   _____

5. No pushing!

   _____

6. Get that radio away from the pool. No radios in the pool area!

   _____

7. Obey the rules! Stop breaking the rules!

   _____

8. Get that dog out of here! No pets allowed!

   _____

9. No eating or drinking in the pool area!

   _____

10. Stop hitting that little boy!

    _____

shallow: not deep.

Look at the following chart on North American etiquette and complete the sentences using *have to*, *don't have to*, and *must not*. The first one is done for you.

North American Etiquette			
	Personal Hygiene	**Introductions**	
		Formal	**Informal**
Necessary	use deodorant wear clean clothes daily	smile shake hands say "Nice to meet you"	smile say "Hello"
Not necessary	wear perfume, cologne	be very serious	shake hands
Prohibited	use too much perfume, makeup	kiss, hug	kiss, hug
	Tipping	**Table Manners**	**Clothing**
Necessary	leave the waiter/waitress a 15 percent tip	wait to eat until everyone is served	wear conservative clothes in business/law/religious services
Not necessary	tip bad waiter/waitress, leave a tip in a fast-food restaurant	accept offers of food	wear conservative clothes in other situations
Prohibited	tip government officials (police, customs)	make noise with mouth when eating	go barefoot* (except at beach)

*Go barefoot: not wear shoes.

(Some information from *Culturgram—United States of America,* Brigham Young University, David M. Kennedy Center for International Studies, 1985.)

1. When you meet someone at a classmate's party, you ___don't have to___ shake hands.

2. North Americans don't have a lot of physical contact with each other, especially with strangers. When you meet someone for the first time, you _____ kiss or hug.

3. To make a good impression at a job interview, you _____ dress conservatively,

   and you _____ put on too much perfume.

4. North Americans like a good sense of humor. Even in business, a person _____

   be formal and serious all the time.

5. For satisfactory service in a restaurant, it is customary to leave a 15 percent tip, but if the service is poor, you _____ tip the waiter.

6. To be accepted in North American society, you _____ take a bath every day, use deodorant, and wear clean clothes.

7. You _____ go barefoot to a church, mosque, synagogue, or temple.

8. A business executive _____ shake hands when he meets someone for the first time.

9. On most college and university campuses, a student _____ dress up for classes; in fact, classroom dress is very casual.

10. Direct eye contact is important for North Americans. You _____ look at them directly and smile when you meet them, or they might think you're dishonest.

▶ **EXERCISE 6**   *(Focus 5, page 175)*

Using the chart from Exercise 5 as a guide, write your own sentences about customs in your native country. Use *have to, don't have to, must,* and *must not.*

NECESSARY

1. _____

_____

2. _____

_____

3. _____

_____

NOT NECESSARY

4. _____

_____

5. _____

_____

6. _____

_____

PROHIBITED

7. _____

_____

8. _____

_____

9. _____

_____

▶ **EXERCISE 7** *(Focus 6, page 178)*

Using the information from the chart in Exercise 5, complete the following conversation about Mary's trip to North America. Use *must, must not, have to,* or *don't have to,* in the present, past, or future tense. The first one has been done for you.

José: Maria, how was your trip to America? You were there all summer, right?

Maria: Yes, I went there with an exchange program. I stayed with a family. It was great!

José: What was it like? Is it true that Americans ____have to____ take two showers a day or they don't feel clean?

Maria: No, that's not true.

José: Is it true that they are informal?

Maria: Yes. While I was there, I **(1)** _____ wear a dress or a skirt. Every day I wore shorts and sneakers, except on the day when we went to court. The father of the family

is a lawyer, and he says that in a courtroom, you **(2)** _____ dress more formally.

José: How was the food? Is it true that they eat hamburgers and hot dogs every day?

Maria: No, that's not true, but in the morning I **(3)** _____ eat cereal and drink American coffee.

José: Was it safe to drink the water, or **(4)** _____ boil the water before drinking it?

Maria: The water was very safe to drink.

José: Was the family rich?

Maria: No, they were middle class. They didn't have servants, so I **(5)** _____ help

around the house. I **(6)** _____ clean my own room and help with the dishes.

There was yard work, but I **(7)** _____ help with that.

José: What else **(8)** _____ do?

Maria: I **(9)** _____ walk the dog.

José: Is it true that in North America you **(10)** _____ treat pets almost like people?

Maria: Yes, the dog was a member of the family. The mother of the family said to me, "Maria,

dogs are our friends. We **(11)** _____ love and respect them."

José: How about the people? Is it true that the people are nice?

Maria: Oh, yes! But one time I'm afraid that I offended some friends of the family. I asked a

woman about her salary. The family told me, "Maria, you **(12)** _____ ask
about a person's salary, age, or weight. It's too personal."

José: I'd like to go next summer. What **(13)** _____ do?

Maria: Well, first, you **(14)** _____ get an application form and fill it out. I'll help you.

► **EXERCISE 8**   *(Focus 6, page 178)*

Exchange your answers to Exercise 6 with a partner (preferably someone from a different
country and culture). Now imagine that you are planning a trip to that person's
hometown. Write sentences about your plans, using *have to/don't have to, will have
to/won't have to,* or *must*. Share your answers with the class.

NECESSARY

1. _____

_____

2. _____

_____

3. _____

_____

NOT NECESSARY

4. _____

_____

5. _____

_____

6. _____

_____

PROHIBITED

7. _____

_____

8. _____

_____

9. _____

_____

UNIT 12

EXPRESSING LIKES AND DISLIKES

▶ **EXERCISE 1**   *(Focus 1, page 186)*

The students in Norma's class have a lot in common. Complete the following sentences about them, using *too* or *either*.

▶ **EXAMPLE:** Her son doesn't eat vegetables, and my daughter <u>doesn't either.</u>

   1. Ramon studies Spanish, and Maria Jose _____

   2. I don't understand Greek, and my friends _____

   3. Ann doesn't like liver, and her sister _____

   4. Cheryl loves animals, and her children _____

   5. Elizabeth loves the English language, and my friends _____

   6. Maria doesn't like to write in English, and Dora _____

   7. Gennadiy listens to classical music, and I _____

   8. She doesn't listen to rock and roll, and I _____

   9. I like the teacher's new haircut, and the other students _____

  10. Roberto doesn't like it, and David _____

▶ **EXERCISE 2**   *(Focus 2, page 186)*

Copy the sentences from Exercise 1, changing *too* and *either* to *so* and *neither*.

▶ **EXAMPLE:** Her son doesn't eat vegetables, and neither does my daughter.

   1. _____

   2. _____

3. _____

4. _____

5. _____

6. _____

7. _____

8. _____

9. _____

10. _____

▶ **EXERCISE 3** *(Focus 3, page 187)*

Correct the mistakes in the following sentences.

1. Scott lives in Iowa, and so is Debbie.
2. I don't know how to windsurf, and my brother doesn't neither.
3. Sung can't type, and neither Fathi can.
4. Mark went to the wrong restaurant, and Alonzo didn't too.
5. Bob didn't go sailing, and either did Irene.
6. Mayumi hasn't been here long, and Sato isn't either.
7. Cynthia was in class yesterday, and you was too.
8. You were sick last week, and neither was Sheila.
9. Lee won't come with us, and either will Ed.
10. Maureen has a cute boyfriend, and so has Patty.

Read the following dialogue between coworkers. Match the sentences in the first column with the appropriate short phrase in the second column. The first one has been done for you.

1. _B_ Oliver went to the union meeting last night.

2. ___ His boss wasn't there.

3. ___ My boss thinks everything is fine at work.

4. ___ He wasn't happy to hear about the meeting.

5. ___ He hasn't been very professional.

6. ___ I felt bad about what he said to us.

7. ___ I think it's wrong not to say what you think.

8. ___ Well, I'm for the union.

9. ___ My boss doesn't like unions.

10. ___ My manager won't be happy if we vote for a union.

11. ___ Oliver can do what he wants.

A. I am too.

B. I did too.

C. My boss, Mr. Fagin, does, too.

D. Mr. Fagin hasn't either.

E. Mr. Fagin wasn't either.

F. Neither does Mr. Fagin.

G. Neither was Mr. Fagin!

H. Neither will Mr. Fagin.

I. So can I!

J. So did I.

K. So do I.

Complete the conversation below with short phrases showing agreement (for example, *so do I/I don't either*) or hedges *(kind of/sort of)*. Use correct capitalization.

IN WRITING CLASS

1. **Brian:** Did the teacher like your composition?

   Daniel: Well, _____.

2. **Brian:** What grade did you get?
   Daniel: I got a C.

3. **Brian:** _____. Actually, I'm happy. I don't usually pass.

   Daniel: _____. I'm terrible at writing. I like conversation, though. I'm better at speaking.

4. **Brian:** _____. How about reading? Do you like reading class?

   Daniel: _____. I don't really like the teacher.

5. **Brian:** _____.

   Daniel: I'm tired of studying English.

6. **Brian:** _____.

   Daniel: I like my other classes a lot better.

7. **Brian:** What other classes?

   Daniel: I'm taking music classes.

8. **Brian:** Really? _____! I'm taking Music Theory and guitar lessons. How about you?

   Daniel: I'm taking theory and voice lessons. Who's your theory teacher?

9. **Brian:** Professor Kaplan.

   Daniel: Do you like the class?

10. **Brian:** _____. It's difficult. I like the other class better. Do you like your voice lessons?

    Daniel: _____. I like Music Theory better. It's my favorite class.

▶ **EXERCISE 6**   *(Focus 6, page 192)*

In Unit 7 there is an exercise on right- and left-brain preferences. The list below shows some additional characteristics of "right-brain" and "left-brain" people. Check (√) the sentences that are true for you. Then add up the number of check marks in each column to see if you are left-brain dominant, right-brain dominant, or balanced. Are your results the same as before?

After you finish, put a circle around all the gerunds in the lists and underline the infinitives.

Left-Brain	Right-Brain
____ I have a place for everything and a system for doing things	____ I enjoy swimming.
____ I enjoy sewing.	____ I enjoy skiing.
____ I enjoy chess.	____ I enjoy bicycling.
____ I understand contracts, instruction manuals, and legal documents.	____ I am good at thinking up new ideas.
____ I like to plan and arrange the details of a trip.	____ I enjoy photography.
____ I like to collect things.	____ I can understand charts and diagrams.
____ I enjoy working on home improvements.	____ I like to relax and just do nothing.
	____ I enjoy dancing.
	____ I like to paint or sketch.

Left-Brain	Right-Brain
____ I enjoy writing.	____ I postpone making telephone calls.
____ I play bridge.	____ I enjoy fishing.
____ I like to read.	____ I enjoy running.
____ I play a musical instrument.	____ After meeting a person for the first time I remember the person's face.
____ I enjoy doing crossword puzzles.	____ When shopping, I buy what I like.
____ After meeting a person for the first time, I remember the person's name.	____ I like to sing in the shower.
____ Before buying something, I read the label and compare prices.	____ I enjoy rearranging my furniture and decorating my home.
____ I'm good at speaking.	
____ I like competing with others.	
____ **Total**	____ **Total**

(From "Orientations Inventory," University Associates, *The 1988 Annual: Developing Human Resources*, pp. 60–63.)

Are you a left-brain person or a right-brain person? _____

How many gerunds did you circle? _____

How many infinitives did you underline? _____

▶ **EXERCISE 7**   *(Focus 6, page 192)*

Complete the following sentences. Use a gerund or infinitive in your answer.

▶ **EXAMPLE:** I hate _____ironing_____.

1. _____ is one of my hobbies.

2. I enjoy _____ and _____.

3. I love _____.

4. I hate _____.

5. I'm good at _____.

6. When I was a little boy/girl, _____ was something that I loved to do.

7. On my vacations, I like _____.

8. I feel good after I finish _____.

9. _____ is something I always postpone doing.

10. _____ and _____ are two Olympic sports I watch.

▶ **EXERCISE 8**   *(Focus 6, page 192)*

Working in groups of three or four, compare your answers to Exercises 6 and 7. Take turns reading statements about yourself. If you agree with someone, say *I do too* or *so do I*. If you disagree, say *I don't either* or *neither do I*.

EXERCISES FOR THE TOEFL® TEST

Units 10–12

Choose the *one* word or phrase that best completes each sentence.

1. I don't like shopping, and Nancy _____.
   - (A) doesn't either
   - (B) doesn't too
   - (C) isn't either
   - (D) isn't neither

2. Bobby has a pair of skates, and _____.
   - (A) Irene has too
   - (B) Irene is too
   - (C) so does Irene
   - (D) so has Irene

3. Kelly _____ to go fishing, and so does Mike.
   - (A) does like
   - (B) doesn't like
   - (C) is like
   - (D) likes

4. Robin loved the movie, and _____.
   - (A) I loved too
   - (B) I didn't
   - (C) so did I
   - (D) so do I

5. Bart enjoys _____ antiques.
   - (A) collect
   - (B) collects
   - (C) collecting
   - (D) to collect

6. In North American classrooms, the students _____ stand when the teacher enters the room.
   - (A) don't have to
   - (B) haven't got
   - (C) not must
   - (D) no should

7. In some classes, students may eat, but they _____ smoke; it's the law.
   - (A) don't have to
   - (B) haven't got
   - (C) mustn't
   - (D) shouldn't

8. During class the teacher can have something to drink, and the students _____.
   - (A) will too
   - (B) are too
   - (C) can too
   - (D) drink too

9. However, students _____ stand up and walk around the class while the teacher is talking.

        (A) oughtn't to   (C) shouldn't

        (B) have to   (D) will have to

10. When I was a student, I _____ treat my teachers with more respect than students do nowadays.

        (A) didn't have to   (C) had to

        (B) had got to   (D) must have

11. _____ do anything to prevent heart disease?

        (A) Have got I   (C) Should I

        (B) Ought I to   (D) Had better I

12. The Heart Association gives some advice: you _____ eat healthy food, without too much fat or cholesterol.

        (A) should   (C) had better not

        (B) must   (D) could

13. If you don't want to die of heart disease, you _____ have a low-fat diet, get more exercise, and get frequent checkups from a doctor.

        (A) shouldn't   (C) could

        (B) had better   (D) had better not

14. If you feel chest pains, you _____ see a doctor as soon as possible, or your life may be in danger.

        (A) could   (C) must

        (B) had better not   (D) ought to

15. Finally, you _____ try to eliminate stress.

        (A) don't have to   (C) couldn't

        (B) shouldn't   (D) could

Identify the _one_ underlined word or phrase that must be changed for the sentence to be grammatically correct.

16. Frank hasn't seen that new movie about skiing, and I haven't neither.
      A   B   C   D

17. After he finish washing the dishes, Fred wants to go for a bike ride. So do I.
      A   B   C D

18. I can understand why he loves working with computers, and his mother can't either.
     A   B   C   D

19. Hilda enjoys to be outside in her yard gardening, and Florence does too.
           A   B   C   D

20. She stays in good physical shape by jogging and to run. Her boyfriend does too.
                          A   B   C   D

21. I think that if a person lives in North America, he or she should learn how to swim.
                                                                                    A
When my parents were in college, they must to pass a swimming test to graduate.
              B   **C**   **D**

22. But at most colleges nowadays, a student doesn't have to do that as a requirement for
                                                              A   **B**
graduation. You're right, I didn't had to do that when I was in college.
                          C   **D**

23. Ought I learn to be safe around water? Yes, you should. You ought to take water safety
        A   **B**   **C**
classes from the Red Cross. The first rule in water safety is that you shouldn't swim
                                                                                D
alone.

24. The second rule in water safety is that to save a drowning person, you mustn't try to
                                                                                        A
swim to him. You ought to throw something. You also could to reach for the drowning
                          B   **C**   **D**
person with something like a pole or towel.

25. Children should learn about water safety. They have to go near the water alone; an adult
              A   **B**   **C**
should always be with them.
        D

26. I have a toothache. What I should do? Well, you could take some aspirin, but it is
        A   **B**   **C**
probably better to see the dentist.
                    D

27. I know I had better not be afraid to go to the dentist, but I always get nervous sitting in
                          A   **B**   **C**
the dentist's chair.
              D

28. The dentist makes me feel anxious, and so does his assistant. Let me see what it looks
                          A   **B**   **C**
like. Oh, that tooth looks painful, and so the tooth next to it.
                                          D

29. You must see the dentist right away! To avoid painful toothaches, you could brush your
        A **B**   **C**
teeth and use dental floss.
              D

30. You ought to visit a dentist twice a year, and your children should so.
        A   **B**   **C** **D**

PRESENT PERFECT

Since and *For*

▶ **EXERCISE 1**   *(Focus 1, page 198)*

Below are some important events in the life of Carmen Alvarez. Decide whether each is a past event, a present event, or an event that began in the past and has continued to the present. Write the sentences under the correct category head. The first one has been done for you as an example.

She has volunteered at the hospital since she moved to New Mexico.

She is studying at the University of New Mexico.

She wanted to be a doctor when she was a child.

She has studied at the University of New Mexico for three years.

She wants to be a doctor.

She moved to New Mexico.

She has wanted to be a doctor since she was a child.

She began studying at the University of New Mexico three years ago.

She is volunteering at the hospital.

PAST

1. _____

2. _____

3. _____

PRESENT

1. _____

2. _____

3. _____

BEGAN IN THE PAST AND CONTINUES NOW

1. <u>She has volunteered at the hospital since she moved to New Mexico.</u>

2. _____

3. _____

► **EXERCISE 2**   *(Focus 1, page 198)*

Using Exercise 1 as a model, write sentences about events in your own life.

PAST

1. _____

2. _____

3. _____

PRESENT

1. _____

2. _____

3. _____

BEGAN IN THE PAST AND CONTINUES NOW

1. _____

2. _____

3. _____

► **EXERCISE 3**   *(Focus 2, page 200)*

Before you can donate blood, you must answer several questions about your medical history. Complete the following dialogue between a blood donor and an interviewer, using the correct form of each verb in parentheses in the present perfect. The first one has been done for you.

Fifth Annual
Blood Drive

Give for the
Heart of It!

Interviewer: How long ___<u>has it been</u>___ (it be) since you ate?

Donor: I _____ (not eat) anything since breakfast.

Interviewer: _____ (you give) blood before?

Donor: Yes, I _____ (give) blood many times.

Interviewer: Really? How long _____ (it be) since you last donated blood?

Donor: I _____ (not donate) blood for a year.

Interviewer: _____ (you have) any serious illnesses?

Donor: No, I _____ (not have) any illnesses.

Interviewer: _____ (you be) in the hospital in the past five years?

Donor: No, I _____ (not be) hospitalized.

Interviewer: _____ (you travel) abroad?

Donor: Yes, I _____ (go) to South America.

Interviewer: How long ago was that?

Donor: I was in South America in 1990, but I _____ (live) in the United States since then.

Interviewer: Thanks for answering the questions. Now please roll up your sleeve.

▶ **EXERCISE 4**   *(Focus 2, page 200)*

Copy the interviewer's main questions from the previous exercise.

1. _____

2. _____

3. _____

4. _____

5. _____

6. _____

Take turns role-playing the interview with a partner. Answer the questions using your own experiences and history.

Complete the following dialogue by putting *since* or *for* in each blank. The blank in the sign in front of the castle has been filled in for you as an example.

Count Dracula: Good evening, Mr. Stoker. Welcome to the Count Dracula Blood Bank. So nice of you to come. We would like to take your blood, but first we want to see if you're our type. Would you answer a few questions?

Stoker: Well, uh, I guess so.

Count Dracula: How long has it been _____ you arrived in Transylvania?

Stoker: I just arrived. I've been here _____ only two hours.

Count Dracula: Oh! Have you had time to explore the castle?

Stoker: Well, I've walked around a little _____ I got here. The castle is interesting, but that back room is full of bats.

Count Dracula: Yes, we've had that problem _____ the castle was built. That reminds me, how long has it been _____ you flew at night?

Stoker: What? I haven't flown at night _____ last year. I'm afraid of the dark.

Count Dracula: Well, perhaps we can help you with that problem. How long has it been _____ you've been in a cemetery?

Stoker: These are the strangest questions I've ever heard. I guess the last time was in March. Yes, it's been three months _____ I was in a cemetery.

Count Dracula: Very good. Finally, Mr. Stoker, have you given blood before?

Stoker: Yes, but I haven't donated _____ at least six months.

Count Dracula: Wonderful! Because you've answered all our questions, we've decided you're a perfect victim—I mean candidate. Please roll down your collar.

Look at the personnel file for Mercy Hospital. Which doctor has worked at the hospital the longest? Which nurse?

Doctors	First Year Employed	Nurses	First Year Employed
Dr. Doolittle	1973	Nurse Candystripe	1975
Dr. Faust	1981	Nurse Nightingale	1973
Dr. Freud	1988	Nurse Ratchet	1967
Dr. Jekyll	1978	Nurse Shark	1984
Dr. Livingston	1969		
Dr. Moreau	1958		
Dr. Spock	1988		
Dr. Zhivago	1973		

Mercy Hospital — Personnel File

23

Use the information from the personnel files to make statements with the words given below.

► **EXAMPLE:** Dr. Zhivago / since Dr. Zhivago has worked at Mercy Hospital since 1973.

1. Dr. Moreau / for _____

_____

2. Dr. Jekyll / since _____

_____

3. Dr. Zhivago and Nurse Nightingale / for _____

_____

4. Dr. Faust / for _____

_____

5. Nurse Ratchet / for _____

_____

6. Dr. Doolittle / since _____

_____

7. Dr. Spock / for _____

_____

8. Nurse Candystripe / for _____

_____

9. Nurse Shark / since _____

_____

10. Dr. Livingston / since _____

_____

11. Dr. Freud and Dr. Spock / since _____

_____

▶ **EXERCISE 7**   *(Focus 5, page 204)*

Rewrite the sentences using the present perfect and *since* or *for*. Remember that the present perfect cannot be used with all verbs.

▶ **EXAMPLE:** She works at the hospital. She began working there six years ago.

   <u>She has worked at the hospital for six years.</u>

1. Lisa started taking that medicine in 1997. She still takes it today.

_____

2. Do you want to be a surgeon? Did you want to be a surgeon when you were a child?

_____

3. Larry is an X-ray technician. He began this career in 1989.

_____

4. My stomach doesn't hurt anymore. It stopped hurting when I took the medication.

_____

5. Joe delivers flowers to the hospital every day. He began delivering flowers two years ago.

_____

6. Sylvia knows my doctor. They met at a hospital fundraiser.

_____

7. It isn't raining; it stopped raining at 5:00.

_____

8. Doug arrived at the hospital thirty minutes ago. The doctor is still in the room with him.

_____

9. Medical technology was improving in the last century. It is still improving.

_____

10. She doesn't take X-rays anymore. She stopped taking X-rays in 1995.

_____

PRESENT PERFECT AND SIMPLE PAST

Ever and Never, Already and Yet

▶ **EXERCISE 1** *(Focus 1, page 214)*

Decide whether each of the following verbs should be in the simple past or the present perfect. Then circle the correct form.

Captain Michael Johnson, one of the best commercial airline pilots in the world, is retiring this year. He **(1)** began / has begun working for Western Airlines 35 years ago. In the beginning of his career, he **(2)** flew / has flown only domestic flights, but later on, the company **(3)** told / has told him to fly internationally. Captain Mike, as the flight attendants call him, **(4)** flew / has flown around the world many times. He **(5)** met / has met a lot of people and **(6)** saw / has seen a lot of different places. In one year he **(7)** went / has gone to India, Egypt, and Greece, where he **(8)** saw / has seen the Taj Mahal, the pyramids, and the Acropolis. In addition, he **(9)** did / has done a lot of exciting things. On one trip, in 1980, he **(10)** jumped / has jumped from an airplane with a parachute, and on another trip he **(11)** rode / has ridden in a submarine. But his life **(12)** wasn't / hasn't been easy. In 1976 his plane almost **(13)** crashed / has crashed; he **(14)** had / has had to make an emergency landing. Ten years ago, he **(15)** had / has had cancer, but Captain Mike **(16)** fought / has fought the cancer and **(17)** won / has won. All in all, he **(18)** was / has been very blessed and so **(19)** did / have we here at Western Airlines. We're going to miss you, Captain Mike.

▶ **EXERCISE 2** *(Focus 2, page 217)*

Have you ever done any of the following things? Using the words below and the present perfect, write questions and answers about your experiences. If you haven't done the activity, use *never* or *not + ever*.

▶ **EXAMPLE:** eat ants

Q: <u>Have you ever eaten ants?</u>

A: <u>Yes, I have.</u>

OR

A: <u>No, I haven't ever eaten ants./No, I've never eaten ants.</u>

1. find a wallet in the street

Q: _____

A: _____

2. fly in a helicopter

Q: _____

A: _____

3. fight in a war

Q: _____

A: _____

4. break a bone

Q: _____

A: _____

5. give blood

Q: _____

A: _____

6. meet a famous person

Q: _____

A: _____

7. have a car accident

Q: _____

A: _____

8. wear snowshoes

Q: _____

A: _____

9. ride a camel

Q: _____

A: _____

10. see a penguin

Q: _____

A: _____

▶ **EXERCISE 3**　　*(Focus 3, page 218)*

Using the verbs from Exercise 2, ask a North American whether he or she has ever done those activities. If he or she has, ask the appropriate questions about the activity (*when*, *where*, etc.). Write all of the answers.

1. _____

_____

2. _____

_____

3. _____

_____

4. _____

_____

5. _____

_____

6. _____

_____

7. _____

_____

8. _____

_____

9. _____

_____

10. _____

_____

Max is going to take another trip abroad. His friend Martha is asking him questions about the trip. Using the words and pictures below, write Martha's questions in the present perfect. Be careful—the verbs need to be changed.

► **EXAMPLE:** already / you / camera / have / for / buy / your?

<u>**Have you already bought film for your camera?**</u>

1. agent / yet / / have / your / travel / you?

_____

2. buy / already / you / ticket / your / / have?

_____

3. a(n) / ever / ticket / on / a / you / lose / have / trip /   ?

_____

4. reservations / have / already / / you / your / make?

_____

5. you / / yet / pack / your / have?

_____

6. yet / you / a /  / find / sitter / have?

_____

7.  / already / your / get / you / have?

_____

8. already / for / you / applied /  / a / have?

_____

9. change / your / yet / you / have /  ?

_____

10. 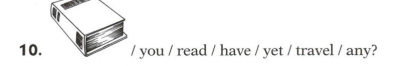 / you / read / have / yet / travel / any?

_____

11. / you / miss / a / ever / have?

_____

12. someone / airport / ever / / else's / at / you / the / take / have?

_____

PRESENT PERFECT
PROGRESSIVE

▶ **EXERCISE 1**   *(Focus 1, page 228 and Focus 2, page 229)*

Match the pictures with phrases from the list. Write sentences that give explanations for the situation using the present perfect progressive. The first one has been done for you as an example.

lift boxes   sit in the sun   unpack dishes   move furniture   sleep
swim   move into new house   look for shells   have nightmares   dream

1. He has been having nightmares.

2. _____

3. _____

4. _____

5. _____

6. _____

7. _____

8. _____

_____

9. _____

_____

10. _____

_____

▶ **EXERCISE 2**   *(Focus 2, page 229)*

Look at the pictures in Exercise 1 and ask your partner questions about the pictures using the present perfect progressive.

▶ **EXAMPLE: A:** *What has he been doing?*
B: *He's been having a nightmare.*

▶ **EXERCISE 3**   *(Focus 2, page 229)*

Work in groups of three. Using the cues, ask one group member questions about what he or she has been doing since coming to class. Then tell the third group member. Take turns asking the questions and telling the person's answers to the third group member.

▶ **EXAMPLE:** speak only English
A: *Have you been speaking only English since you came to class?*
B: *Yes, I've been speaking only English.*
A: *(to other group member) She has been speaking only English.*

1. speak only English
2. talk to classmates
3. study grammar
4. do exercises
5. read in English
6. listen to the teacher
7. whisper to friends
8. sing in English
9. take notes

Using the given time frame as a cue, think of an activity that you have been doing and continue to do today. Write a sentence for each.

► EXAMPLE: since last year

    <u>I have been living on my own since last year.</u>

1. since last year

    _____

2. since the beginning of the semester

    _____

3. for the past week

    _____

4. since I started learning English

    _____

5. for the past two years

    _____

6. since my last birthday

    _____

7. since last weekend

    _____

8. since last winter

    _____

9. for the past two weeks

    _____

10. since last night

    _____

Fill in each blank with the appropriate form of the verb in parentheses. The first one has been done for you as an example.

Joel: Jimmy, you look terrible. What __have you been doing__ (you do) recently?

Jimmy: I _____ (not sleep) well lately.

Joel: _____ (you feel) sick?

Jimmy: I _____ (not feel) sick. My allergies _____ (bother) me for the past week or so.

Joel: _____ (something, happen) recently at school that is bothering you?

Jimmy: Well . . . not really.

Joel: What _____ (worry) you?

Jimmy: I _____ (think) about my grammar exam for the past couple of days.

Joel: Why?

Jimmy: We _____ (study) the present perfect progressive recently, and I'm not sure I understand it.

Joel: _____ (you study) hard and _____ (ask) for help when you need it?

Jimmy: Yes, I _____ (memorize) the form of the present perfect progressive, and I _____ (try) to use it whenever I speak English.

Joel: Sounds like you don't have anything to worry about. I'm sure you'll do fine.

Fill in each blank with the present perfect or present perfect progressive as appropriate. The first one has been done for you as an example.

For years I __have read__ (read) a book right before I go to sleep. Recently, I **(1)** _____ (read) biographies. I read biographies of Charlie Chaplin and Mahatma Gandhi, and for the past couple of nights I **(2)** _____ (read) about Christopher Columbus.

I **(3)** _____ just _____ (realize) that Mom's sixtieth birthday is coming up soon, and it **(4)** _____ (be) a long time since we did something for her birthday. I think we should do something special this year.

What do you suggest?

Well, recently, I **(5)** _____ (collect) some pictures of us as children. I thought if we got some more pictures we could make a nice collection.

Mom used to get up at 6:30 every morning, but now she's on vacation, and she **(6)** _____ (wake up) at 7:30. It is only one hour, but it makes a big difference. She **(7)** _____ (have) more energy since she **(8)** _____ (be) on vacation.

George just returned from Japan. He **(9)** _____ (work) there for the past two months. Over the past year his company **(10)** _____ (set up) a new branch in Tokyo.

EXERCISES FOR THE TOEFL® TEST

Units 13–15

Choose the *one* word or phrase that best completes each sentence.

1. _____ to the Great Smokies National Park since it was improved?
   - (A) Have you been gone
   - (B) Did you went
   - (C) Have you gone
   - (D) Did you go

2. No, but I _____ to go there next summer.
   - (A) has wanted
   - (B) have been
   - (C) wants
   - (D) want

3. I _____ there; I returned last night.
   - (A) have just been camping
   - (B) have been camping there just
   - (C) just have been camping there
   - (D) have camped

4. I _____ in such a beautiful park since I was in Yellowstone National Park.
   - (A) no stayed
   - (B) haven't stayed
   - (C) haven't staied
   - (D) don't stay

5. The forest and mountains are beautiful, but the campsites are rough. They _____ all the comforts of home.
   - (A) haven't had
   - (B) hadn't
   - (C) don't have
   - (D) haven't

6. How _____ the park?
   - (A) have they improved
   - (B) they have been improving
   - (C) they have improved
   - (D) have they been improved

7. Recently, the Park Service _____ more campsites.
   - (A) have added
   - (B) has been adding
   - (C) is adding
   - (D) have been adding

8. For many years, the park rangers _____ more hiking trails.
   - (A) has developed
   - (B) have been developed
   - (C) developed
   - (D) have been developing

9. Rangers have protected the natural beauty of the Great Smokies National Park _____ it was created.

    (A) for   (C) since

    (B) when   (D) that

10. In the past twenty years, computers _____ an important part of everyday life.

    (A) have become   (C) have became

    (B) has become   (D) have becomed

11. We _____ computers move into the workplace, schools, and homes since the invention of the microchip.

    (A) have saw   (C) have been seeing

    (B) have seed   (D) have seen

12. _____ computers have become more important, it has become more important to be computer literate.

    (A) When   (C) For

    (B) Since   (D) At the time

13. Almost every part of our lives _____ computerized over the past two decades.

    (A) have been   (C) has been doing

    (B) has been   (D) have been doing

14. Since I _____ in college, I _____ a computer to help me with my assignments.

    (A) 've been being . . . 've   (C) 've been . . . 've been using

        been using

    (B) was . . . 've used   (D) 've been . . . used

15. Yesterday I _____ a computer to write my term paper.

    (A) have used   (C) was used

    (B) used   (D) have been using

Identify the *one* underlined word or phrase that must be changed for the sentence to be grammatically correct.

16. Where have you been? I have seen not you around here lately.
             A   B   C   D

17. I've just been visiting my brother since the past two weeks. He lives in Anchorage, Alaska.
   A B   C   D

18. Anchorage, Alaska? Why were you visiting Anchorage in the middle of the winter? What
                                 A   B

have you be doing there for two weeks?
   C   D

19. Winter in Alaska is fun. I have been skiing and ice skating. Also I seen a dog sled race.
                         A   B   C   D

20. Have you never seen a dog sled race? No, I haven't.
   A   B   C   D

21. The native people of Northern Canada and Alaska have been participating in dog sled
                                                        A   **B**   **C**
races since more than 500 years.
         D

22. I found out that the Inuit people has been using dog sleds as their main method of
                                    A   **B**
transportation since they settled in North America.
              C   **D**

23. The dogs have pulled sleds during the winter for hundreds of years. They have carryed
              A   **B**   **C**   **D**
people and equipment across the frozen land.

24. In the past, every Inuit family has been having a dog sled team because it was their only
         A   **B**   **C** **D**
source of transportation.

25. Since the invention of the snowmobile, dog sleds has become less popular for
         A   **B**   **C**
transportation; however, dog sled races are still a popular sport during the cold winters.
                                    D

26. The men or women who race dog sleds are "mushers." For many years before the race,
                                                            A
they have been trained their dogs to pull the sled and to work together as a team.
     B   **C**   **D**

27. One of the most famous dog sled races is the Iditarod Trail. It covers more than 1,000
                                                                    A
miles of Alaskan wilderness. This race had challenged mushers and their dogs for many
                                          B   **C**   **D**
years.

28. You have ever slept outside in the middle of winter? Mushers and their dogs sleep in
         A   **B** **C**   **D**
snow camps during the race.

29. My brother have watched the start of the Iditarod Trail race several times, but he hasn't
                    A   **B**   **C**
ever watched the finish.
         D

30. Last week, I saw this great race for the first time. I watched the beginning of the race in
         A   **B**   **C**
Anchorage, and then I have flown to Nome, Alaska, to see the finish.
                              D

31. It was exciting to watch the dogs and the mushers cross the finish line. All of the people
    A   **B**

have been shouting to encourage the musher and his dogs.
   C   **D**

32. I haven't known that Alaskan winters were so exciting. You have really had a great
       A   **B**   **C**   **D**

vacation.

UNIT 16

MAKING OFFERS WITH WOULD YOU LIKE

▶ **EXERCISE 1**   *(Focus 1, page 240)*

Pierre Eclair has just become the new assistant manager of the Gourmet Diner. He is trying to make the atmosphere a little more polite and sophisticated, so he is listening to how the waitresses talk to their customers. Read the dialogue between Wanda the waitress and her customers, Phil and Emily. Then rewrite the dialogue using polite forms. The first one has been done for you as an example.

Wanda: Good morning. Where do you want to sit? *Good morning. Where would you like to sit?*

Wanda: Do you want a table by the window? _____
Phil: Yes, that would be fine.

Wanda: Do you want some coffee? _____
Phil: Yes, please, two cups of coffee.

Wanda: Sugar or cream in your coffee? _____
Phil: Sugar for me, please . . .
Wanda: Here's your coffee.

Wanda: Do you want to order now? _____
Phil: Yes, I guess we do.

Wanda: What do you want? _____
Emily: I'll have eggs and French toast.

Wanda: How do you want your eggs? _____
Emily: Fried, but not too well done.

Wanda: Do you want me to tell the cook to make them over easy? _____

_____
Emily: Yes, please.

Wanda: And you, sir? Do you want eggs, too? _____

_____

Phil: Yes, I'll have the cheese omelet with hash browns.

Wanda: Do you want anything else? _____

Phil: Yes, some orange juice.

Wanda: Great. I'll be back with your breakfast in a moment.

▶ **EXERCISE 2**   *(Focus 3, page 242)*

Read the description of the conversations between Marc Antony and Cleopatra on their first date, and then on another date a year later. Write the dialogues using *would you like* **or** *do you want,* **as appropriate. Marc Antony's first line has been written for you as an example.**

First Date

MARC ANTONY	CLEOPATRA
1. asks Cleopatra for a date	**2.** accepts the offer
3. asks Cleopatra what kind of restaurant she wants to go to	**4.** says she prefers French or Italian
5. asks what movie Cleopatra wants to see	**6.** tells him which movie she wants to see

Marc Antony: 1 _Would you like to go out with me this weekend?_____

Cleopatra: 2. _____

Marc Antony: 3. _____

Cleopatra: 4. _____

Marc Antony: 5. _____

Cleopatra: 6. _____

One Year Later

MARC ANTONY	CLEOPATRA
7. asks Cleopatra if she wants to stay home and watch the football game	**8.** says she prefers to go country-western dancing
9. asks if she wants to order out for pizza	**10.** says she prefers Chinese food
11. asks her if she wants to go bowling and eat at the bowling alley instead	**12.** she accepts

Marc Antony: **7.** _____

Cleopatra: **8.** _____

Marc Antony: **9.** _____

Cleopatra: **10.** _____

Marc Antony: **11.** _____

Cleopatra: **12.** _____

▶ **EXERCISE 3** *(Focus 3, page 242)*

Write a dialogue for each of the following situations. Be sure to consider the politeness level of the situation. If the offer is refused, give a reason for the refusal. The first dialogue has been started for you. Explain why you choose to make the polite request formal or informal.

1. A flight attendant on an airplane offers a passenger lunch. The passenger isn't hungry but would like something to drink.

Flight Attendant: Would you like some lunch?

Passenger: _____

_____

Explanation: <u>The flight attendant would use a formal request because her job is to</u>

<u>serve the passenger and she does not know him personally.</u>

2. A father offers to help his son with his homework. The son really needs help.

_____

_____

Explanation: _____

_____

3. The attendant in a gas station offers to wash a car windshield. The driver accepts.

_____

_____

Explanation: _____

_____

4. A woman with two small children and many packages is trying to get on a bus. You offer to help her. She accepts.

_____

_____

Explanation: _____

_____

5. An elderly man is standing at the corner. He looks lost. Another man offers to help him. The elderly man explains that he is waiting for his son.

_____

_____

Explanation: _____

_____

6. Your friend visits you on a hot summer day. You offer her a glass of lemonade. She gladly accepts.

_____

_____

Explanation: _____

_____

7. Your father's friend is in your city for a couple of days. You offer to show him the sights. He is not able to accept your offer because he has to attend a business meeting.

_____

_____

Explanation: _____

_____

8. Deb's husband has a headache. She offers to get him some aspirin. He accepts.

_____

_____

Explanation: _____

_____

▶ **EXERCISE 4**   _(Focus 3, page 242)_

Below are situations in which you might make a request. Work with a partner and write dialogues for each situation. Act out some of the dialogues for your classmates.

▶ **EXAMPLE:** On a subway train

   Those packages look heavy. Would you like me to hold them for you? Yes, thanks. It's

   hard to stand up on the train and hold them.

1. Someone is sick _____

_____

2. On the first day at a new school _____

_____

3. At a restaurant _____

_____

4. In a department store _____

_____

5. At a picnic _____

_____

6. At a travel agency _____

_____

UNIT 17

REQUESTS AND PERMISSION

Can, Could, Will, Would, and May

Below are some situations in which requests are commonly made. For each situation, write a request using *can*, *could*, *will*, *would*, or *may*, as appropriate.

▶ **EXAMPLE:** You're driving to a party with a friend. You're not sure exactly where the party is, but you have a map in the glove compartment. You say to your friend:

Could you please look for a city map in the glove compartment? I'm not exactly sure

where the party is.

1. You aren't sure which bus goes to the beach. You see a man waiting at the bus stop. You say:

   _____

   _____

2. After you find out which bus to take, you want to know how often it stops here. You ask the man:

   _____

   _____

3. When you come home from shopping, your arms are full of packages. You see your neighbor near the front door of your apartment building. You say:

   _____

   _____

4. You have to be at work a half hour early tomorrow. Your husband/wife always gets up before you and wakes you up. You say to him or her:

_____

_____

5. You are looking for your seats in a theater. You see an usher and ask:

_____

_____

6. You forgot to buy milk when you went to the grocery store. Ask your roommate to stop and get some.

_____

_____

7. You're giving a dinner party. Suddenly you realize you are out of eggs, which you need for your dessert. You phone your neighbor and ask:

_____

_____

8. You're trying to find the immigration building. You know it's nearby. You approach a woman and say:

_____

_____

9. You see the kind of cake mix you want to buy on the top shelf, but you can't reach it. You ask another customer to reach the box for you.

_____

_____

10. Your friend is playing the guitar and singing at a party. Ask him or her to sing your favorite song:

_____

_____

Imagine someone asked you the polite requests below, but you must refuse the request. Use a softening phrase.

► **EXAMPLE:** Can you lend me your notes from the last class?

   I'm sorry, I can't. I left my notes at home today.

1. Could you help me with this math problem? _____

   _____

2. May I borrow a dollar? _____

   _____

3. Would you please help me get my ball down from the tree? _____

   _____

4. My car has a flat tire. Will you please help me change it? _____

   _____

5. May I please have some more orange juice? _____

   _____

6. Mom, will you please help me practice my lines for the play? _____

   _____

7. My car is broken. Can you please give me a ride tomorrow? _____

   _____

8. If you are going out, would you please return my library books? _____

   _____

9. Please make copies of these documents. _____

   _____

Hana is a flight attendant. Passengers often make requests of her. Following are some requests the passengers have made. Write Hana's response to each request, varying the responses.

► **EXAMPLE:** Could you help me put this bag in the bin? <u>Sure, I would be happy to.</u>

1. Could you get me a pillow? _____

_____

2. Would you bring me some more sugar for my coffee, please? _____

3. Can you show me where the bathrooms are?

_____

_____

4. May I have another drink? _____

_____

5. Will you take away my food tray? _____

_____

6. Can you tell me where to catch my connecting flight? _____

7. May I have a deck of cards, please? _____

8. Would you get me a magazine? _____

9. Will you turn down the air conditioning? I can't reach it. _____

10. May I have some earphones? _____

Below are some situations where a person might ask for permission. For each situation, write a permission question. Use *would, may,* or *do (would) you mind if,* as appropriate.

▶ **EXAMPLE:** You get a chance to meet your favorite singer. Ask for permission to take his or her picture.

   Would you mind if I took your picture?

1. A young girl wants to spend the night at a friend's house this weekend. She asks her mother for permission.

   _____

   _____

2. Gus is at a formal dinner party and needs to leave the table for a minute. He asks the hostess for permission.

   _____

   _____

3. You are at a friend's house. You would like to smoke, but you're not sure whether it is allowed. Ask permission to smoke.

   _____

   _____

4. You have a friend coming from Japan to visit. You'd like your friend to see what an American school is like. Ask permission from your teacher to bring your friend to class.

   _____

   _____

5. Your community organization is having a special summer program for children. Ask the owner of the drugstore for permission to put one of your posters about the program in his store window.

   _____

   _____

6. You have a doctor's appointment at 4:00. Ask your boss for permission to leave work early.

   _____

   _____

7. Your classroom is getting a little hot and stuffy. Ask your teacher for permission to open the window.

_____

_____

8. You find an interesting magazine at the library. You're not sure whether you can check out magazines. Ask the librarian for permission to check the magazine out.

_____

_____

9. You park your car by an office building. You are not sure whether parking is permitted. Ask the security guard for permission to park there.

_____

_____

10. You need to visit your counselor. Ask permission from your teacher.

_____

_____

▶ **EXERCISE 5**   *(Focus 5, page 256)*

Below are the reactions of each person who was asked permission for something in Exercise 4. Use the information from Exercise 4 and the information below to write appropriate responses. If permission is refused, use a softening phrase and tell why the request is refused.

▶ **EXAMPLE:** The singer says "yes."

Sure, you can take my picture. _____

1. The girl's mother says no.

_____

2. The hostess says yes.

_____

3. Your friend doesn't allow smoking in the house.

_____

4. Your teacher says yes.

_____

5. The owner gives permission.

_____

134   UNIT 17

6. Your boss doesn't give permission.

_____

7. Your teacher says yes.

_____

8. The librarian says no.

_____

9. The security guard says no.

_____

10. Your teacher says yes.

_____

UNIT 18

USED TO WITH STILL AND ANYMORE

▶ **EXERCISE 1**   *(Focus 1, page 264)*

Read the following statements. Circle T if the statement is true and F if it is false.

T F   **1.** People used to use candles and gas lamps because they didn't have electricity.

T F   **2.** Before electricity, people used to put a big block of ice in the icebox; today we use a refrigerator.

T F   **3.** Before electricity, people used to use batteries for power.

T F   **4.** Before the invention of the car, people used to ride the bus.

T F   **5.** People used to walk much more than they do now.

T F   **6.** There didn't used to be as much violent crime as there is now.

T F   **7.** People used to know much more about nutrition than they do now.

T F   **8.** Big families used to be much more common than they are now.

T F   **9.** People used to live longer than they do now.

T F **10.** There didn't used to be a big drug problem.

▶ **EXERCISE 2**   *(Focus 2, page 265)*

Using the words below, ask and answer questions with the correct form of *used to*.

▶   You / have long hair? <u>Did you used to have long hair?</u>

      <u>Yes, I used to have very long hair.</u>

  1. Where / you / live? _____

     _____

  2. When you were a little boy or girl, what / you / play? _____

     _____

3. When you were in elementary school, what / you / do after school? _____

_____

4. When you were very young, / your parents / read to you? _____

_____

5. What bad habit / you / have? _____

_____

6. What / you / look like? _____

_____

7. Who / be / your best friend? _____

_____

8. You / live in the city or the country? _____

_____

9. Where / you / go on vacation? _____

_____

10. You / wear glasses? _____

_____

▶ **EXERCISE 3**   *(Focus 3, page 265)*

Fill in each blank with the correct form of *used to* or *anymore*.

My grandmother complains about how things have changed, and she says that life

(1) _____ be better.

Families aren't families the way they **(2)** _____ be. Everyone's divorced. If

a husband and wife are having problems with their marriage, they don't stay together

(3) _____. And mothers **(4)** _____ stay home and take care of their

children, but not **(5)** _____. Everyone's working. No one has time for children

(6) _____.

And the cars! No one walks **(7)** _____; everybody drives. We **(8)** _____

walk five miles to school every day, even in the winter. And in school, the children don't have to think **(9)** _____. In math class, for example, we **(10)** _____ add, subtract, multiply, and divide in our heads. Kids don't use their heads **(11)** _____; they use calculators.

Computers have taken control over our lives. In my day, we didn't have computers. We didn't even have electricity. My mother **(12)** _____ spend all day cooking in the kitchen. Nobody eats home-cooked food **(13)** _____. Food **(14)** _____ taste better. It's all chemicals and preservatives now.

And people don't talk to each other **(15)** _____. They're too busy to talk, too busy to eat, too busy to think. . . .

Life **(16)** _____ be simple, but it isn't **(17)** _____.

▶ **EXERCISE 4**   *(Focus 4, page 266)*

Read each statement. Circle T if the statement is true and F if it is false.

T   F   **1.** There used to be a country called the Soviet Union, but there isn't anymore.

T   F   **2.** There's still a country called Italy.

T   F   **3.** Thomas Jefferson used to be president of the United States, and he still is.

T   F   **4.** They still haven't found the city of Atlantis.

T   F   **5.** Antony and Cleopatra used to float down the Nile River, and they still do.

T   F   **6.** They used to speak Icelandic in Ireland, and they still do.

T   F   **7.** There used to be a wall separating East Germany from West Germany, and there still is.

T   F   **8.** Alaska used to belong to Russia, but it doesn't anymore.

T   F   **9.** The Taj Mahal used to be in India, and it still is.

T   F   **10.** There didn't used to be a country named Uzbekistan, and there still isn't.

Holly and Greta have been friends since high school. Greta just went to their 20-year high school reunion, but Holly couldn't go. In the following dialogue, they are talking about their former classmates. Look at the pictures and complete the dialogue, using the correct form of each verb in parentheses and *still* or *anymore*. Be careful—many of the sentences are negative.

Jim

20 YEARS AGO   **TODAY**

Holly: Did you see Jim Jensen? He used to be so wild!

Greta: Yes, but he _____ (be). He looks very conservative now.
Holly: Was he thin in high school? I don't remember.

Greta: Yes, and he _____ (be).

Holly: _____ (he, wear) glasses?
Greta: Yes, he does.

Holly: _____ (he, play) the guitar?

Greta: Yes, he does, but now he plays classical guitar. He _____ (play) rock and roll

_____ .

Holly: Didn't he used to have long hair?
Greta: Yes, he did, but now he's bald. I also saw Jan Bissing at the reunion. Remember her?
She used to be the most popular girl in school.

Jan

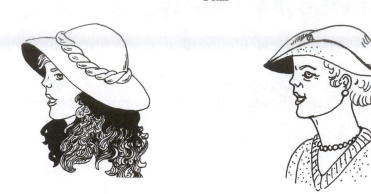

20 YEARS AGO	TODAY

Holly: What does she look like now? _____ (she, look) the same?

Greta: Yes, except for her hair. She _____ (have) long, brown hair _____.

It's short and blonde. And she _____ (be) cute! She _____ (have) those big blue eyes and those thick eyelashes.

Holly: There was something different about her . . . didn't she always used to wear a hat?

Greta: Yes, and she _____ (do).

Holly: Didn't she used to date George Weissler?

Greta: She _____ (do)! In fact, they're going to get married next month.

▶ **EXERCISE 6**   *(Focus 5, page 268)*

Look at the information in the chart on the next page and answer the questions in complete sentences, using *still, anymore,* or an adverb of frequency. Be careful with verb tenses.

Carol used to be single. Last year she married George. George was divorced and has two children. The chart shows how Carol's life has changed.

	Before	**Now**
always	go dancing on weekends	stay home on weekends
often/usually	go out to eat travel	cook dinner clean the house do the laundry every day
sometimes	read novels go to the beach	help kids with homework go to the beach read novels
seldom/hardly ever	cook clean	go out to eat
never	stay home on weekends go to baseball games have children	go dancing travel

1. Before she got married, how often did Carol used to go dancing?

   _____

2. Does Carol still read novels?

   _____

3. Does Carol ever help the kids with their homework?

   _____

4. When she was single, what did Carol often used to do on her vacation?

   _____

5. Did Carol ever used to cook and clean?

   _____

6. Does Carol ever cook and clean now?

   _____

7. Does Carol still go dancing?

   _____

8. Does she still go to the beach?

   _____

9. Does she go out to eat every night?

   _____

10. How often does she do the laundry?

   _____

EXERCISES FOR THE TOEFL® TEST

Units 16–18

Choose the *one* word or phrase that best completes each sentence.

1. Would you carry this notebook for me? Sure, I _____.
   - (A) can
   - (B) could
   - (C) will
   - (D) may

2. _____ lend me your calculator? I left mine at home.
   - (A) May you
   - (B) Would you
   - (C) Would you like
   - (D) Might you

3. _____ but the batteries in my calculator have gone dead. It doesn't work.
   - (A) Yes,
   - (B) Sure,
   - (C) No problem,
   - (D) I'd like to,

4. I used to do my assignments by myself, _____.
   - (A) but I don't do that anymore
   - (B) but I still do that
   - (C) and I still do that
   - (D) and I don't do that anymore

5. I _____ frustrated when I wasn't sure of the correct answer.
   - (A) may be
   - (B) used to
   - (C) used to be
   - (D) use to be

6. _____ to compare your answers with mine? That way we could both check our homework.
   - (A) Do you like
   - (B) Would you like
   - (C) May you like
   - (D) Could you like

7. That's a great idea. _____ you move your desk over here so we can compare answers?
   - (A) May
   - (B) Do
   - (C) Would
   - (D) Did

8. _____ you mind if I skip the movies tonight? I have a headache.
   - (A) Could
   - (B) Will
   - (C) Would
   - (D) May

9. The dog looks thirsty. _____ some water?
  (A) Would you mind
  (B) Would they like
  (C) Want
  (D) Does it want

10. _____ work downtown?
  (A) Did you used to
  (B) Did you use to
  (C) Do you used to
  (D) Do you use to

Identify the one underlined word or phrase that must be changed for the sentence to be grammatically correct.

11. Would you help me, please? I'm trying to get to South Mall. You can tell me what bus I
  A   B   C
  should take?
  D

12. You can't get a bus to downtown from here. Do you like me to show you the way to the
  A   B   C   D
  bus stop?

13. Yes, please, could you show me the way? I use to know where all the buses stopped, but I
  A   B   C
  haven't taken a bus in a long time.
  D

14. No problem. The buses to downtown don't stop here still. You could take either the 3 or
  A   B   C
  the 16 bus. The bus stop is there, across the street.
  D

15. May you help me? Sure. What do you need? Could you please reach that jar on the top
  A   B   C   D
  shelf? It's too high for me.

16. May I borrow your pencil? Yes, you would. Thanks. No problem.
  A   B   C   D

17. Want some help with that? No thanks. I'm used to do it by myself.
  A   B   C   D

18. I used to go the whole night without sleep, but anymore I can't do that.
  A   B   C   D

19. Would you like to be meeting my uncle? He's very funny. He used to tell us jokes all night,
  A   B   C
  and I think he still tells great jokes.
  D

20. Should you help me find my car keys? I can't find them anywhere. I'm sorry I can't help
  A   B   C
  you now. I'm late for work, but I could ask Celia to help you find them.
  D

PAST PERFECT

Before and *After*

▶ **EXERCISE 1**   *(Focus 1, page 274)*

Read about Jerry and then fill in the time line on page 145 with information from Jerry's life. Include only the underlined verbs. The first one has been done for you.

   Jerry Zimmerman used to be a typical young man. Then, five years ago, a car accident changed his life forever. The accident paralyzed him, and now he's in a wheelchair.

   After the accident, Jerry was in the hospital for a long time. He had a lot of operations. He had never been in the hospital before, and he had never seen so many doctors: surgeons, anesthesiologists, neurologists . . . He had never felt so much pain; he was sure the physical therapists were experts in torture. He had to learn to get around in a wheelchair, too.

   Before the accident, Jerry had played tennis and sailed. Now he's learning to play table tennis, and he still sails his boat on the lake near his house. He also competes in races in his wheelchair. He had always had a dog, but after the accident, he needed a specially trained dog to help him around the house. Last year he got Connie, a black Labrador.

   As for his love life, Jerry had been engaged* to a woman named Debbie. He's still going to be married, but now he's engaged to Patty—his physical therapist.

   Engaged: having a formal agreement to get married.

BEFORE ACCIDENT	AFTER ACCIDENT	NOW
1. Jerry had never been in the hospital.	1. Jerry was in the hospital.	1. He's in a wheelchair.
2.	2.	2.
3.	3.	3.
4.	4.	4.
5.	5.	5.
6.		
7.		

► **EXERCISE 2** *(Focus 2, page 274)*

A reporter is interviewing Jerry (Exercise 1) for a feature story about people with disabilities. The reporter wants to know what Jerry's life was like before he was paralyzed. Using the words given below, write the reporter's questions and Jerry's answers. Use the past perfect.

► **EXAMPLE:** your life / pretty normal?

Had your life been pretty normal? Yes, it had.

1. How many times / you / be in the hospital / before the accident?

2. What sports / you / play / before the accident?

3. you / run in races?

_____

_____

4. Before Connie, / you / have a dog?

_____

_____

5. you / be engaged to Patty?

_____

_____

▶ **EXERCISE 3** *(Focus 2, page 274)*

Combine each of the following pairs of statements to make one sentence, using the word in parentheses to connect them. Change one of the verbs into the past perfect. The first one has been done for you.

1. He had a fight with his wife.
Allen slept badly last night. (because)

Allen slept badly last night because he had had a fight with his wife.

_____

2. He slept late this morning.
Nobody set the alarm. (because)

_____

_____

3. Allen didn't have any clean underwear.
Nobody did the laundry. (so)

_____

_____

4. Nobody went grocery shopping.
There wasn't any coffee. (because)

_____

_____

5. Allen forgot to go to the gas station.
There wasn't any gas in the car. (because)

_____

_____

6. He was very worried.
His boss told him not to be late anymore. (so)

_____

_____

7. He looked in the mirror and saw that he didn't comb his hair.
He was driving. (while)

_____

_____

8. He realized that he didn't cash his paycheck.
He got to the gas station. (when)

_____

_____

9. Allen found that he left his wallet at the gas station.
He got to work. (as soon as)

_____

_____

10. He realized that he forgot it was Saturday.
He noticed there were no cars in the parking lot. (when)

_____

_____

▶ **EXERCISE 4**   *(Focus 3, page 277)*

In each of the following sentences, write 1 over the action that occurred first and 2 over the second action. If there are three verbs, write 3 over the third action. Then check (√) the sentences in which it is necessary to use the past perfect to indicate the order of events. The first one has been done for you.

                       1   2
1. ____ Last night Mr. Wilson walked the dog and then let the cat out.

2. ____ He locked the doors, turned off the lights, and went upstairs.

3. ____ When he got upstairs, he realized that he had forgotten to take out the garbage.

4. ___ He went back downstairs and took out the garbage.

5. ___ When he went upstairs to brush his teeth, he heard a noise.

6. ___ By the time he got to the door, the noise had stopped.

7. ___ Mr. Wilson went back upstairs and heard the noise again. It sounded like someone crying.

8. ___ He went back downstairs, and again, by the time he reached the door, the noise had stopped.

9. ___ By that time, Mr. Wilson had gone up and down the stairs so many times that he was dizzy. He went to bed.

10. ___ The next morning when Mr. Wilson went outside to get the newspaper, he saw what had caused the noise the night before.

11. ___ He was surprised to see that the cat had had kittens.

▶ **EXERCISE 5**   *(Focus 3, page 277)*

Answer the following questions about Mr. Wilson (Exercise 4) with complete sentences. The first one has been done for you.

1. Did Mr. Wilson walk the dog last night?

   Yes, he walked the dog.
   _____

2. What had Mr. Wilson done by the time he locked the doors and turned off the lights?

   _____

3. What was he doing when he first heard the noise?

   _____

4. What did Mr. Wilson do when he heard the noise?

   _____

5. Why did he first go back downstairs?

   _____

6. Did Mr. Wilson hear the noise before or after he went upstairs?

   _____

7. Why did he feel dizzy?

   _____

8. By the time he went to bed, how many times had Mr. Wilson walked up the stairs?

   _____

9. What had caused the noise?

_____

For each verb in parentheses below, write the correct tense (simple past, past perfect, present perfect, simple present, or present progressive). If there's another word in parentheses, include it in your answer. The first one has been done for you.

Last winter Yarima Good **(1)** _____took_____ (take) a trip into the past. She

(2) _____ (go) to visit her people in South America, the Yanomama, one of the most

primitive cultures on Earth.

Yarima **(3)** _____ (go) from the Stone Age to the twentieth century six years ago.

Before then, she **(4)** _____ (wear, never) clothes or **(5)** _____ (be) in shoes.

Since then, she **(6)** _____ (learn) to make light with a little plastic thing on the wall.

She **(7)** _____ (learn, also) not to be afraid of mirrors or toilets or cars.

Anthropologist Kenneth Good first **(8)** _____ (visit) South America in 1975. He

(9) _____ (be) the first *nabuh,* or outsider, Yarima **(10)** _____ (see, ever).

Yarima **(11)** _____ (be) a child then; she **(12)** _____ (be) fourteen years old.

Ken **(13)** _____ (stay) with the Yanomama people for twelve years. As a child, Yarima

(14) _____ (fish) with him in the river; then she **(15)** _____ (grow) up. They

(16) _____ (fall) in love and **(17)** _____ (get) married.

Now Yarima **(18)** _____ (be) the stranger, the *nabuh,* living in a place where

everything **(19)** _____ (be) different. She **(20)** _____ (have) three children,

and because of them, she **(21)** _____ (have) to live in this new world outside of

New York City. For the Yanomama, the only counting system is *one, two,* and *many,* so Yarima's

tutor **(22)** _____ (teach) her to count. Yarima **(23)** _____, (learn) but

it **(24)** _____ (be, not) easy.

Ken Good **(25)** _____ (write) a book about his Amazon adventure, *Into the Heart.*
(Based on "Stone Age to Suburbs" by Nancy Shulins, Associated Press, *Miami Herald,* January 3, 1992.)

UNIT 20

ARTICLES

The, A/An, Some and Ø

▶ **EXERCISE 1** *(Focus 1, page 286)*

Read the story in which nouns are underlined. Write D above the nouns with definite articles and I above the nouns with indefinite articles. The first one has been done for you.

Rigoberta Menchu is a Guatemalan Indian woman. In 1993 she won the Nobel Peace Prize for her work for the Indians of Guatemala.

In the book, *I Rigoberta Menchu,* she tells her life story and talks about the customs and ceremonies of the Quiche Indians. She begins by telling about how, as a young girl of eight, she helped her family by working on a coffee plantation. It was hard work to pick the coffee beans and weed the coffee plants.

Most of the story tells how the army tried to control the Indians by taking property and killing many Indians. Rigoberta's father, mother, and one of her brothers were killed by soldiers.

Rigoberta has tried to fight the violence with peace. She has worked with an organization that has tried to bring peace and justice to the Guatemalan Indians.

Complete the following story by putting *a*, *an*, or *the* in each blank, as appropriate. The first one has been done for you.

A Fractured Fairy Tale

One morning Papa Bear, Mama Bear, and Baby Bear couldn't eat their porridge because it was

too hot. So _____*the*_____ three bears went for **(1)** _____ walk while their porridge

cooled. While they were gone, Goldilocks came in. She saw **(2)** _____ porridge cooling.

First, she tried Papa's bowl, but **(3)** _____ porridge was too hot. Next, she tried Mama's

bowl, but **(4)** _____ porridge was too cold. Finally, she tried Baby Bear's porridge, and

it was just right, so she ate it all up.

After that, Goldilocks was tired, so she looked for **(5)** _____ place to rest. She found

(6) _____ bedrooms. She tried Papa's room, but **(7)** _____ bed was too hard.

Then she tried Mama's bed, but it was too soft. Finally, she tried Baby's bed, and it was just right.

She felt so comfortable that she fell asleep.

When **(8)** _____ bears came home, they found **(9)** _____ big surprise.

Papa Bear looked at **(10)** _____ spoon in his bowl and said, "Someone has been eating

my porridge."

Mama Bear looked at **(11)** _____ spoon in her bowl and said, "Someone has been

eating **(12)** _____ porridge, all right."

When he looked at his bowl, Baby Bear began to cry; **(13)** _____ bowl was empty.

When Mama went to her bedroom, she found **(14)** _____ blankets in a mess.

"Look, Papa, **(15)** _____ beds are a mess."

"You're right," Papa Bear agreed. "Someone has been sleeping in my bed, too."

"Here she is!" shouted Baby Bear.

At the sound of Baby Bear's voice, Goldilocks jumped up and ran out.

However, **(16)** _____ police officer was near **(17)** _____ bears' house. Goldilocks was arrested. She was charged with unlawful entry, stealing porridge, and bad manners. **(18)** _____ judge sent her to Miss Manners' School of Etiquette for three months.

▶ **EXERCISE 3**   *(Focus 3, page 289*

Complete this story by filling the blanks with either *a, an,* or Ø (zero). The first one has been done for you.

High-Wire Orangutans

Have you ever seen _____*an*_____ orangutan swinging above you? At the National Zoo in Washington, D.C., the orangutans go from their home in the great ape house to

(1) _____ special orangutan school called the Think Tank. Zookeepers don't take the apes to the Think Tank. The orangutans get there on their own. **(2)** _____ high tower stands in the orangutan yard at the great ape house. **(3)** _____ cables connect the tower to five other towers. If he wants, **(4)** _____ adventurous orangutan can travel across the cables. On each tower there is **(5)** _____ platform where the orangutans can take **(6)** _____ rest. **(7)** _____ electrified set of wires beneath the platform keeps the orangutans from going below. Swinging along the cables, **(8)** _____ orangutans can see **(9)** _____ ornamental duck pond and **(10)** _____ people walking below. This is **(11)** _____ unique experience for the orangutans. No other zoo has such **(12)** _____ facility.

(13) _____ modern zoos are different from the zoos of just twenty years ago. In the past, **(14)** _____ animals were shut in small cages. Today zoos are encouraging animals to use their natural talents. Now **(15)** _____ animals have more **(16)** _____ freedom.

▶ **EXERCISE 4**   *(Focus 5, page 291)*

Complete the following story by filling each blank with *a*, *an*, *the*, or *some*, as appropriate. The first one has been done for you.

On a cool fall day, _____*a*_____ grasshopper

sat on **(1)** _____ stone and watched

(2) _____ ants put away **(3)** _____

food that they had collected during **(4)** _____

summer.

"Do you have any food to share with

(5) _____ hungry grasshopper?" he asked.

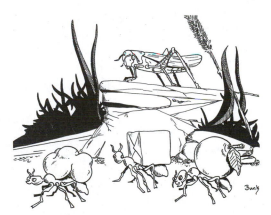

(6) _____ ants stopped working. They looked at **(7)** _____ grasshopper.

"What were you doing all summer?" asked **(8)** _____ ant with **(9)** _____ apple on his back. "Didn't you gather any food?"

"No, I didn't have time to gather food," answered **(10)** _____ grasshopper.

"What were you doing?" **(11)** _____ ant asked.

(12) _____ grasshopper replied, "I was singing **(13)** _____ songs and practicing **(14)** _____ new dances."

"Songs and dances won't help you this winter," said **(15)** _____ ant. Then **(16)** _____ ants turned away and left **(17)** _____ grasshopper.

▶ **EXERCISE 5**   *(Focus 6, page 292)*

Complete the following story by filling each blank with *the* or Ø (zero). The first one has been done for you.

Newfoundland is one province of Canada that attracts _____Ø_____ tourists of all ages. Much of **(1)** _____ province is on Newfoundland Island and is separated from Canada's mainland. **(2)** _____ ferries and **(3)** _____ airplanes bring **(4)** _____ passengers from all over **(5)** _____ world. **(6)** _____ rugged coast of this island is full of **(7)** _____ natural beauty.

(8) _____ tourists marvel at **(9)** _____ inlets in Gros Morne National Park.

(10) _____ nature is everywhere on Newfoundland Island. **(11)** _____ people watch for **(12)** _____ birds such as **(13)** _____ eagles, **(14)** _____ cormorants, and **(15)** _____ gillemots, or they look for **(16)** _____ pilot whales. Yes, **(17)** _____ life is beautiful on Newfoundland Island.

Complete this weather report by filling each blank with *a, an,* or *the*. **The first one has been done for you.**

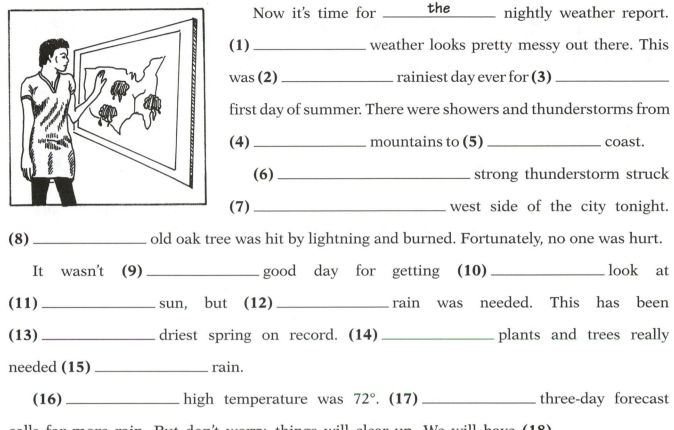

Now it's time for _____the_____ nightly weather report. **(1)** _____ weather looks pretty messy out there. This was **(2)** _____ rainiest day ever for **(3)** _____ first day of summer. There were showers and thunderstorms from **(4)** _____ mountains to **(5)** _____ coast.

(6) _____ strong thunderstorm struck **(7)** _____ west side of the city tonight.

(8) _____ old oak tree was hit by lightning and burned. Fortunately, no one was hurt.

It wasn't **(9)** _____ good day for getting **(10)** _____ look at **(11)** _____ sun, but **(12)** _____ rain was needed. This has been **(13)** _____ driest spring on record. **(14)** _____ plants and trees really needed **(15)** _____ rain.

(16) _____ high temperature was 72°. **(17)** _____ three-day forecast calls for more rain. But don't worry, things will clear up. We will have **(18)** _____ excellent weekend.

A RTICLES WITH
N AMES OF P LACES

▶ **EXERCISE 1**   *(Focus 1, page 304)*

Read the description of Canada on the next page. Circle the geographical names that do not take articles and underline the geographical names that take articles. The first one has been done for you.

Canada

Canada is the northernmost country in North America. Canada is bordered by the United States on the south, the Arctic Ocean on the north, the Atlantic Ocean on the east, and the Pacific Ocean and Alaska on the west. Canada is divided into ten provinces and two territories. Quebec is the largest province, and Prince Edward Island is the smallest province. The two largest cities in Canada are Montreal and Toronto. The two highest mountains in Canada are Mount Logan and Mount St. Elias, which are located in the Rocky Mountains. The Great Lakes are part of Canada's southern border. Lake Huron is the largest lake in Canada. The most important rivers in Canada are the St. Lawrence River and the Mackenzie River.

▶ **EXERCISE 2**   *(Focus 1, page 304)*

Write a paragraph about the geography of your native country. If necessary, use an encyclopedia for help with specific facts. Include information about rivers, lakes, deserts, mountains, cities, states or provinces, and neighboring countries.

▶ **EXERCISE 3**   *(Focus 1, page 304)*

Test your knowledge of world geography. Name a geographical location for each category that begins with the letter at the top of the column. Be sure to include articles for the places that require them.

	M	G	S
Rivers			
Deserts			
Cities			
Lakes			

	H	A	R
Islands and island chains			
Mountain chains or peaks			
Streets in your city			

	P	M	N
States or provinces			
Planets			
Oceans or seas			

► **EXERCISE 4**   *(Focus 2, page 307)*

Complete the following story by writing *the* or Ø in each blank, as appropriate. The first one has been done for you.

In 1952, Hurricane Andrew destroyed more property than any other natural disaster in the United States. Not only did it destroy homes and businesses, but also, many public institutions were damaged.

All of the colleges and universities in the area were damaged. _____Ø_____ Barry University and **(1)** _____ St. Thomas University were only slightly damaged, but **(2)** _____ University of Miami and **(3)** _____ Florida International University were heavily damaged.

Two national parks, **(4)** _____ Everglades National Park and **(5)** _____ Biscayne National Park, were destroyed. Many animals that lived in those parks lost their homes. In other parks, including **(6)** _____ Oleta River Park and **(7)** _____ Greynolds Park, some trees blew down, but they were not damaged too much.

In downtown Miami, most of the historical buildings, like **(8)** _____ Freedom Tower, escaped much damage. Also, most of the hospitals, like **(9)** _____ Mount Sinai Hospital, **(10)** _____ Jackson Hospital, and **(11)** _____ Baptist Hospital, were able to continue operating throughout the crisis.

South Florida is famous for its tourist attractions, many of which, such as
(12) _____ Seaquarium and **(13)** _____ Parrot Jungle, had to close down
for several months. The most badly damaged attraction was **(14)** _____ zoo.

South Florida recovered quickly from the devastating hurricane. If you visit there today, you'll
see very few signs of the destruction.

EXERCISES FOR THE TOEFL® TEST

Units 19–21

Choose the *one* word or phrase that best completes each sentence.

1. I like fruit. I had _____ banana and _____ apple for lunch.
   - (A) the . . . the
   - (B) a . . . a
   - (C) an . . . a
   - (D) a . . . an

2. _____ your assignment before class started?
   - (A) Had you finished
   - (B) When you finished
   - (C) Do you finish
   - (D) You had finishing

3. _____ famous mountains in North America is Mt. St. Helens, which erupted in 1980.
   - (A) One of most
   - (B) One of the most
   - (C) The most
   - (D) The more

4. The tallest building in the United States is _____, which is located in _____.
   - (A) Sears Tower . . . Chicago
   - (B) the Sears Tower . . . Chicago
   - (C) the Sears Tower . . . the Chicago
   - (D) Sears Tower . . . the Chicago

5. We _____ in the ocean before we went to California.
   - (A) had never swam
   - (B) have never swum
   - (C) hadn't swam
   - (D) had never swum

6. I like the theater. I would like to see _____ more plays.
   - (A) the
   - (B) a
   - (C) an
   - (D) Ø

7. _____ squid once before that, but it made me sick.
   - (A) I'd eaten
   - (B) I hadn't eaten
   - (C) I've ate
   - (D) I'd like to eat

8. The Rio Grande is the border between _____.
   - (A) the Mexico and the Texas
   - (B) the Mexico and Texas
   - (C) Mexico and the Texas
   - (D) Mexico and Texas

9. Before she _____ in Moscow, she _____ in Kiev.
    (A) had lived . . . lived   (C) lived . . . had lived
    (B) lived . . . lived   (D) lived . . . has lived

10. _____ is the closest planet to _____.
    (A) The Venus . . . the earth   (C) Venus . . . the earth
    (B) Venus . . . an earth   (D) A Venus . . . earth

11. _____ that music before you went to the concert?
    (A) Did you ever heard   (C) Had you ever heared
    (B) Had you ever heard   (D) Had ever you heard

12. The fiftieth state in _____.
    (A) the United States is the   (C) United States is the Hawaii
        Hawaii
    (B) the United States is Hawaii (D) United States is Hawaii

13. That is _____ silliest thing you have ever said. It never snows in Miami.
    (A) the   (C) an
    (B) a   (D) some

14. _____ SUNY, is a large university system in New York.
    (A) The State University   (C) State University of the New York, or the
        of New York, or the
    (B) The State University   (D) State University of New York, or
        of New York, or

15. He _____ her before he saw her at the party.
    (A) already had meet   (C) had already met
    (B) already has met   (D) has already met

Identify the *one* underlined word or phrase that must be changed for the sentence to be grammatically correct.

16. The Philippines are a group of islands located in the South Pacific, north of Indonesia.
         A   **B**   **C**   **D**

17. After I had made my daughter a dress for her birthday, I baked a cake. She loved a dress
   A   **B**   **C**   **D**
because it was silk.

18. I have decided to go to the University of California before I received an acceptance letter
       A   **B**   **C**
from Stanford.
     D

19. Grand Canyon is one of the most popular of all the national parks in North America.
      A   **B**   **C**   **D**

20. Before I left home, my mother had always cooked a big meal for the whole family on the
  $\quad\quad$ A $\quad\quad\quad\quad\quad\quad\quad\quad\quad\quad\quad\quad\quad\quad\quad\quad\quad$ B $\quad\quad\quad\quad\quad$ C
  Sundays.
  $\quad$ D

21. One of the Great Lakes that makes up part of the border between Canada and the United
  $\quad\quad\quad\quad\quad\quad\quad$ A $\quad\quad\quad\quad\quad\quad\quad\quad\quad\quad\quad\quad\quad\quad\quad\quad\quad\quad\quad$ B $\quad\quad\quad$ C
  States is the Lake Superior.
  $\quad\quad\quad\quad$ D

22. Had you eaten Italian food before you had visited Italy?
  $\quad\quad$ A $\quad\quad$ B $\quad\quad\quad\quad\quad\quad\quad$ C $\quad\quad$ D

23. I had eaten pizza before I visited Italy, but I no had eaten Italian spinach pizza.
  $\quad\quad$ A $\quad\quad\quad\quad\quad$ B $\quad\quad\quad\quad\quad\quad$ C $\quad$ D

24. Usually I don't have an large appetite, but we had walked so far that I was starving by the
  $\quad\quad\quad\quad\quad\quad\quad$ A $\quad\quad\quad\quad\quad\quad$ B $\quad\quad\quad\quad\quad\quad$ C
  time we got to the restaurant.
  $\quad$ D

25. At the southern tip of Vancouver Island is <u>the city</u> of the Victoria.
  $\quad\quad\quad$ A $\quad\quad\quad\quad\quad$ B $\quad\quad\quad$ C $\quad\quad$ D

26. I had the problems with the homework. Did you understand the solution for <u>number 5</u>?
  $\quad\quad\quad$ A $\quad\quad\quad\quad\quad$ B $\quad\quad\quad\quad$ C $\quad\quad\quad\quad\quad\quad\quad\quad\quad\quad$ D

27. The biology includes the study of plants and animals.
  $\quad$ A $\quad\quad\quad\quad\quad$ B $\quad\quad$ C $\quad\quad\quad$ D

28. Before I had seen the Alps, I had visited the Andes Mountains in South America.
  $\quad\quad\quad$ A $\quad\quad\quad\quad\quad$ B $\quad\quad\quad\quad$ C $\quad\quad\quad\quad$ D

29. I had not read an assignment before class, so I didn't understand what the professor was
  $\quad\quad$ A $\quad\quad\quad\quad$ B $\quad\quad\quad\quad\quad\quad\quad\quad\quad\quad$ C $\quad\quad\quad\quad\quad$ D
  talking about.

30. One of most interesting school subjects is geography. When I was young, I enjoyed study-
  $\quad\quad\quad$ A $\quad\quad\quad\quad\quad\quad\quad\quad\quad\quad\quad\quad\quad\quad$ B
  ing about mountains, rivers, and different countries.
  $\quad\quad\quad$ C $\quad\quad$ D

UNIT 22

THE PASSIVE

▶ **EXERCISE 1**   *(Focus 2, page 315)*

Complete the following letter, using the appropriate form of the passive voice in the simple past, past perfect, present perfect, or future.

Dear Julie,

The last time I wrote to you my life was very different. Do you remember that Charlie and I were thinking about leaving the city and moving far away? Well, we did it!

Our decision to build our house in the north woods of Canada **(1)** _____ (make) three years ago. The lumber **(2)** _____ (buy) and **(3)** _____ (move) by truck over miles of bad road. The plans for the house **(4)** _____ (draw up) on our dining room table. I was in charge of the work, but my contribution **(5)** _____ (limit) to giving orders. Most of the work was done by professionals, although a lot of the house **(6)** _____ (design) by Charlie. It's fabulous!

The house **(7)** _____ (build) out of native Canadian pine in a large and beautiful field. The field **(8)** _____ (cover) with summer flowers when we arrived. I'm sorry to say that the flowers **(9)** _____ (cut) to make room for the house. Our puppy, Caesar, was very happy with the small doghouse that Charlie built in the backyard. While we were all working on the house, we **(10)** _____ (visit) every day by some of the wild animals

of northern Canada. We gave them names of Walt Disney characters. The deer **(11)** _____ (name) Bambi, the rabbit **(12)** _____ (call) Thumper, and a small grey wolf **(13)** _____ (nickname) Goofy. The skunk in our front yard **(14)** _____ (name) Flower. We built a fence to surround our two dozen acres of land. The house **(15)** _____ (finish) in four months, before the autumn frost, but the inside **(16)** _____ (*not + paint*) until the following spring.

Our furniture **(17)** _____ (send) from the city, and we **(18)** _____ (move) in by Halloween. But the only trick-or-treaters that **(19)** _____ (see) that year were two raccoons, a woodchuck, and a fox.

That was three years ago. . . . Since then we have decided to stay. Our apartment in the city **(20)** _____ (sell), our employers **(21)** _____ (notify) that we're not returning to work (even though Charlie and I **(22)** _____ [*just* + promote] when we decided to move), and we've told all our friends. Soon Charlie and I **(23)** _____ (*both* + employ) by different companies, but we **(24)** _____ (allow) to stay here at home and work by computer.

I thought that it was going to be difficult for the children to adjust, but Jonathan, Lindsey, and Alex **(25)** _____ (*not* + bother) at all by the change. They have made new friends, and they love playing outside every day. I love it because there's no traffic, polluted air, noise, or crime.

Well, Julie, I have to go. You're welcome to come up for a visit anytime.

Love,

Nancy

Read the following report from a local newspaper describing a car accident. As the editor, you have to decide which is more appropriate for each sentence, the active or passive voice, and put a check (✔) next to it. The first one has been done for you.

1. ___ A car accident injured a seven-year-old boy on Wednesday.

   ✔ A seven-year-old boy was injured in a car accident on Wednesday.

2. ___ A bus was hit by the boy's father, Donald Derby, at the intersection of 1st Avenue and Spencer Street.

   ___ The boy's father, Donald Derby, hit a bus at the intersection of 1st Avenue and Spencer Street.

3. ___ A stop sign had been run by Derby.

   ___ Derby had run a stop sign.

4. ___ The boy was thrown through the car window.

   ___ The force of the accident threw the boy through the car window.

5. ___ Derby's daughter, Debbie, 3, was also in the car, but the broken glass did not cut her.

   ___ Derby's daughter, Debbie, 3, was also in the car, but she was not cut by the broken glass.

6. ___ An ambulance took the father to St. Christopher Hospital.

   ___ The father was taken to St. Christopher Hospital.

7. ___ The accident also injured the driver of the bus, Joe Barta.

   ___ The driver of the bus, Joe Barta, was also injured.

8. ___ An ambulance took him to Cedars Hospital, where doctors treated him.

   ___ He was taken to Cedars Hospital, where he was treated.

9. ___ Seat belts were not being worn by the Derbys.

   ___ The Derbys were not wearing seat belts.

10. ___ Derby will be charged with running a stop sign and driving without a license.

    ___ The police will charge Derby with running a stop sign and driving without a license.

Use the cues at the left to make sentences with the *get*-passive. The sentences are to help you decide which tense to use. The first one has been done for you.

Linda is a very busy working mother, but no matter how much work she does, she always gets her housework done, too.

1. clean/house *The house gets cleaned.* _____

2. cook/meals _____

3. do/dishes _____
At this time, many things are being done to improve our city.

4. design/parks _____

5. renovate/historic buildings _____

6. build/housing for poor people _____
Every year our college does general repairs. These are some things that were done last year.

7. paint/classrooms _____

8. plant/trees _____

9. remodel/the cafeteria _____
Many companies are trying to decide how they are going to deal with global competition. Some companies have decided that several changes will be made for next year. What changes will be made?

10. cut/salaries _____

11. lay off/employees _____

12. not hire/new employees _____

Complete the following story with the *be*-passive or the *get*-passive and the past participle of the verb. The first one has been done for you.

A Weird Wedding

Bea Prepared and Larry Lucky got married last week. Some unexpected events happened during Bea and Larry's wedding and honeymoon.

First, one week before the wedding, the minister <u>was transferred</u> (transfer) to a new church, so they had to find a replacement at the last minute. After that, Larry **(1)** _____ (lay off) unexpectedly. Then, on the night before the wedding, Bea **(2)** _____ (poison) from the fish she **(3)** _____ (serve) for dinner.

On the day of the wedding, the flowers **(4)** _____ (not deliver) because the florist **(5)** _____ (lose) on the way to the church. During the ceremony, the organist **(6)** _____ (confuse) and played the funeral march instead of the wedding march. Also, the bride's dress **(7)** _____ (tear) when the groom accidentally stepped on it. Then the ceremony **(8)** _____ (interrupt) when a mouse came running through the church. The bridesmaids **(9)** _____ (scare) and began to scream.

After the wedding ceremony, the reception **(10)** _____ (hold) outdoors, but it started to rain and everyone got wet. Bea and Larry went to Las Vegas for their honeymoon, but their luggage **(11)** _____ (put) on a flight to Hawaii.

▶ **EXERCISE 5** *(Focus 6, page 322)*

Decide if the *by* + agent phrase is always necessary as used in the following essay. Cross out the *by* phrases that you think are unnecessary.

It's that time of year again. Every night, gigantic sea turtles are coming out of the water and up on the beach to lay their eggs. As soon as the turtles lay their eggs, the nests are covered with sand by the turtles, and then they go back into the sea. One of nature's mysteries, they return to the same place every year.

Early every morning before sunrise, marine biologists and volunteers go up and down the beach looking for new nests. The nests are moved by them to a safer, darker area. The reason for

 this is that baby sea turtles are attracted by bright light. If there's a building with bright lights on the beach, the babies will go toward the building instead of going toward the ocean, where they should be going. After the nests are moved by the people, the chances that the turtles will survive are increased by the people.

People can see a sea turtle by participating in a turtle watch between May and August. A turtle watch is held every night by the Department of Natural Resources. Reservations are required by them.

The sea turtle is protected by state and federal laws. People are being warned by officials to stay away from sea-turtle nests. If a person is caught by someone taking or bothering a sea turtle, its eggs, or its nest, that person will be fined $20,000 by the government, and he/she could spend a year in prison. There's a Sea Turtle Hot Line that people should call if a baby turtle is seen by them going away from the ocean.

(Based on "Sea Turtles Hit Beaches in Broward" by Alan Topelson, *Miami Herald,* May 1, 1993.)

PHRASAL VERBS

> ► **EXERCISE 1**   *(Focus 1, page 330)*

Using the pictures as cues, complete each sentence with a phrasal verb. Make sure the verbs agree in person and tense. The first one has been done for you.

1. Yesterday was Saturday, so Patrick _____*got up*_____ late.

2. He (not) _____ his clothes right away.

3. Instead, he _____ in his comfortable chair, read the newspaper, and drank some coffee.

4. Finally he _____ the coffee and got dressed.

5. Maurine is a kindergarten teacher. You might think she has an easy job, but every day

   after school she _____ her own classroom.

6. First, she _____ all of the toys.

7. Then she _____ her lesson plans for the next day.

8. When she finishes everything, she _____ the lights and goes home.

► **EXERCISE 2**   *(Focus 2, page 331)*

Read the story. Then write each underlined phrasal verb next to its meaning below. Number 10 has been done for you as an example.

When I woke up this morning I was glad it was Saturday. Then I remembered that I had homework to do for Monday. Last week my teacher gave me the assignment to find out about burial customs around the world and write up a report about it. I put off doing my research for a whole week. Now I have to hand in my report on Monday. I got out my notebook and my pencil, but then I realized I didn't know anything about burial customs. I put on my clothes and decided that I should go to the public library and look up some information.

On the way to the library I met up with my friend Brittany. She wanted to go out shopping. When I explained what I had to do, she offered to help me out.

1. postpone _____

2. search for _____

3. write _____

4. dress _____

5. assist _____

6. research _____

7. give to a teacher _____

8. encountered _____

9. go _____

10. stopped sleeping ___*woke up*___

11. took from its place _____

Complete each sentence by writing the phrasal verb and the object that best complete the question. The first one has been done for you.

1. Angela _____turns_____ _____on_____ the _____radio_____ .

2. She likes to listen to music while she _____ _____ her

   _____ and _____ _____ the trash.

3. But the music is too loud. Her mother says, "Angela _____ _____

   that _____ !"

4. So Angela _____ _____ the radio and _____

   _____ the _____ .

5. Mr. Smith: "Ms. Falco, I know we _____ _____ a meeting last week

to discuss the contract, but I'm afraid we'll have to _____

_____ the _____ until next week—I have an unexpected
emergency at the office."

6. Ms. Falco: "That's no problem. I'll contact the other members and _____

_____ the _____ for today. Should I _____

_____ another meeting for next week the same time?"

Mr. Smith: "That would be great."

▶ **EXERCISE 4**   *(Focus 4, page 335)*

**Rewrite the sentences in Exercise 3 with the object between the verb and the particle.
The first one has been done for you.**

1. Angela turns the radio on.

   or Angela turns it on.

2. _____

   _____

3. _____

   _____

4. _____

_____

5. _____

_____

6. _____

_____

▶ **EXERCISE 5**   *(Focus 4, p. 335 and Focus 5, p. 336)*

Replace each underlined object with a pronoun. Rewrite the sentences with the pronoun between the verb and the participle *if possible.*

▶ **EXAMPLE:** I just got over a cold, and then I got the flu.

I just got over a cold, and then I got the flu. _____ (inseparable verb, not possible)

Don't throw out all of those newspapers; recycle them!

Don't throw them out; recycle them! _____

1. She was feeling sad, so we tried to cheer up Janet.

_____

2. I called up Janet at work, and I could tell something was wrong.

_____

3. She said she was having a bad day. This morning when she turned on her new TV, nothing happened.

_____

4. She thought she would have to take the TV back to the store.

_____

5. Maybe she could get by with her old TV.

_____

6. This afternoon, I ran into a friend of mine who repairs TVs.

_____

7. He went to Janet's house and went over the TV carefully.

_____

8. Janet said, "I don't want to throw out the TV.

_____

9. My friend found out the problem.

_____

10. He came across a loose wire in the electrical cord.

_____

▶ **EXERCISE 6**   *(Focus 6, page 339)*

For each of the following phrasal verbs, write two sentences using the noun phrases on the right as cues. Separate the verb when possible.

▶ **EXAMPLE:** pick up   it
                        a package at the post office

     *Anne had to pick it up.*_____

     *Anne had to pick up a package at the post office.*_____

    turn off   them
            all the electrical appliances before going on vacation.

1. _____

2. _____

    call up   my family
           them

3. _____

4. _____

    get off   the horse
           it

5. _____

6. _____

    take off   my wet shoes and socks
           my shoes

7. _____

8. _____

    look up   it
           the new address of the movie theater

9. _____

10. _____

run into   her parents
            them

11. _____

12. _____

Take turns with a partner asking and answering the following questions.

1. Where did you grow up?
2. Did you ever show up late for dinner? What did your mother say?
3. Did you ever come home late? Did your parents punish you?
4. How often does your family eat out?
5. What is something that you wanted but got by without when you were a child?
6. What American customs will never catch on in your country?
7. How did you get to school today?
8. Can you fix a car that has broken down?
9. Have you ever passed out?

ADJECTIVE CLAUSES AND PARTICIPLES AS ADJECTIVES

▶ **EXERCISE 1**   *(Focus 1, page 350)*

The following words are used to describe people. Unscramble the words and write complete sentences to finish the description.

▶ **EXAMPLE:** an / in / is / extremist / some / someone / way / who / is

A *fanatic* is someone who is an extremist in some way.

1. a / about / is / likes / other / people / talk / who / to / person

A *gossip* _____

_____

2. ages / and / are / are / between / nineteen / of / people / the / thirteen / who / young

Teenagers _____

_____

3. are / from / money / or / pocket / purse / steal / who / thieves / your

Pickpockets _____

_____

4. are / better / else / everyone / people / than / who / they're / think

Snobs _____

_____

5. alcohol / doesn't / someone / drink / is / who

A *teetotaler* _____

_____

6. everything / is / knows / (s)he / someone / who / thinks

A *know-it-all* _____

_____

7. a / army / has / in / is / lowest / rank / soldier / who / the / the

A *private* _____

_____

8. a / an / individual / is / lot / of / spends / time / TV / watching / who

A *couch potato* _____

_____

9. are / are / elderly / people / who

Senior citizens _____

_____

10. a / a / lazy good-for-nothing / is / guy / who's

A *bum* _____

_____

▶ **EXERCISE 2**   *(Focus 2, page 352)*

Using one word or group of words from each column, write a complete sentence.
Numbers 1–6 are conversational definitions of animals (which means they're informal),
and 7–12 are textbook definitions (which means they're formal). The first one has been
done for you.

CONVERSATIONAL DEFINITIONS

Cockroaches	a big wild animal	people are afraid of
Dogs	a colorful bird	people don't like to see in their home
Piranhas	a wild animal	we call "man's best friend"
The monkey	bugs	we see in hot climates
The parrot	fish	we see living in ice and snow
The polar bear	pets	we see in the jungle, swinging through the trees

1. Cockroaches are bugs that people don't like to see in their homes. _____

_____

2. _____

_____

3. _____

_____

4. _____

_____

5. _____

_____

6. _____

_____

WRITTEN DEFINITIONS

Cockroaches	a mammal	exterminators are constantly trying to eradicate
Dogs	a multicolored	scientists classify as the canine species
Piranhas	bird	scientists have determined to be related to human
The monkey	a primate	beings
The parrot	domestic animals	we call carnivores, or meat-eating animals
The polar bear	fish	we find inhabiting arctic regions
	insects	we find inhabiting tropical jungles

7. _____

_____

8. _____

_____

9. _____

_____

10. _____

_____

11. _____

_____

12. _____

_____

What differences do you see between the formal and informal definitions?

Choose and circle the correct adjectives.

Sandy and Victor, both English teachers, lived abroad for many years, first in Saudi Arabia, and then in the Far East, where, like many **(1)** experienced/experiencing travelers, they suffered from culture shock. Recently they returned to the United States and experienced something called reverse culture shock. They had lived abroad for a very long time, and everything back home was new for them.

The cars seemed so big, and the people did too. Sandy and Victor had forgotten how many overweight Americans there were. But everyone was **(2)** obsessed/obsessing with dieting; people thought about it all the time. Every magazine seemed to have an article about dieting, but not many people seemed **(3)** disciplined/disciplining enough to follow a diet. Most were **(4)** disappointed/disappointing dieters.

When Sandy and Victor had first arrived in Saudi Arabia, it was **(5)** surprised/surprising to see the Arab women **(6)** covered/covering from head to toe. Sandy was equally **(7)** shocked/shocking when she returned to the U.S. and saw women wearing hair rollers in public.

And both Sandy and Victor were **(8)** frustrated/frustrating because they didn't have a car. When they lived abroad, transportation had never been a problem, but the North American city that they lived in had very poor public transportation. Sometimes the couple had to wait an hour for the bus. It was very **(9)** annoyed/annoying. And the bus stop was almost a mile from their apartment, so they had to walk a lot, too. At the end of the day, they were **(10)** exhausted/exhausting.

It's difficult to return home after being in another country for a while. At first, Sandy and Victor were **(11)** worried/worrying that they had a negative attitude about everything, but they felt **(12)** relieved/relieving to hear about reverse culture shock. It will take time for them to feel comfortable living here again.

▶ **EXERCISE 4** *(Focus 3, page 355)*

Have you experienced culture shock? How about reverse culture shock? Write about your own experiences by completing the following sentences. Use the *-ed* or *-ing* form of the words in parentheses, as appropriate. If any of these adjectives don't reflect your own feelings or experiences, feel free to replace them with adjectives that do.

1. I was (surprise) when I first saw _____

2. It was (frustrate) to _____

3. I was (confuse) when _____

4. It was (excite) to _____

5. I was (worry) that _____

6. It was (frighten) when _____

7. It was (fascinate) to see _____

8. I was (embarrass) when _____

9. I was (annoy) when _____

10. I felt (relieve) when _____

UNIT 2 5

CONDITIONALS

► **EXERCISE 1**   *(Focus 1, page 364)*

The following passage is about Constantine, a Romanian immigrant who lives in California and drives a taxi. Fill in the blanks with hypothetical conditionals. Be careful—some are negative.

1. Constantine doesn't really want to live here, but because of political problems, he can't

   live in Romania. If politics _____ (be) different, Constantine _____ (have) to live in another country.

2. Constantine has to live abroad—he can't live in Romania. He _____ (live) in

   his apartment in Bucharest if he _____ (have) to live abroad.

3. Constantine has a hard life in California; life is much easier in Romania. Constantine

   _____ (have) a decent life if he _____ (live) in Bucharest.

4. He doesn't know much English, so he works as a taxi driver. If he _____

   (know) more English, Constantine _____ (work) as an engineer; he

   _____ (work) as a taxi driver.

5. Constantine learned his English on the street. His English is okay, but if he

   _____ (go) to school, he _____ (learn) more English, especially how to read and write.

6. Constantine shares a small apartment with four other Romanians—he can't afford a nice

   place. He _____ (live) in a nice apartment if he _____ (have) a decent job.

7. Constantine's life is even more difficult because he's waiting for political asylum. His life

   _____ (be) easier if he _____ (have) to wait for political asylum—it's been three years.

8. Constantine is not a legal resident of the country, so he can't bring his family here. If he

_____ (be) a resident, he _____ (bring) his family to the United

States.

9. He's not very happy because his family lives so far away. He _____ (be) happier

if he _____ (bring) his family to live here.

10. Constantine's wife is in Bucharest, taking care of the family alone. If she _____

(be) here, she _____ (have) Constantine's help.

▶ **EXERCISE 2**   *(Focus 2, page 366)*

PART A

Interview five North Americans, asking them, "If you could make three wishes, what would they be?"

PART B

Summarize their answers in the following chart.

Answers

PART C

Write a short paragraph summarizing the results of your survey. Were there any similarities among the answers? Were you surprised by any of the answers?

_____

_____

_____

_____

_____

_____

_____

_____

_____

_____

_____

_____

▶ **EXERCISE 3**   *(Focus 3, page 367)*

Complete the following hypothetical conditional sentences.

1. I'd be a millionaire if _____

2. If I had more free time, _____

3. If I were you, _____

4. She would buy that if _____

5. If my house were on fire, _____

6. I'd travel around the world if _____

7. If I could change one thing about my life, _____

8. I wouldn't do that if _____

9. If I could make three wishes, _____

10. I would be a better student if _____

The following people are thinking about their pasts and how different individuals and events changed their lives. The pairs of sentences express what really happened in the past. Write hypothetical conditionals based on these sentences. The first sentence in the pair should be used in the *if* clause.

► **EXAMPLE:** Mary went to the Bahamas on her vacation. That's where she met Gordon.

If Mary hadn't gone to the Bahamas, she wouldn't have met Gordon.

1. Mary met Gordon. That's why she didn't marry her high school sweetheart.

_____

_____

2. Gordon went to medical school. Because of that, he didn't go to law school.

_____

_____

3. Gordon became a doctor. As a result, he didn't become a lawyer.

_____

_____

4. Claudia had Mr. Stack for algebra. Because of him, she passed math and graduated from high school.

_____

_____

5. Mr. Stack was Claudia's teacher. As a result, Claudia didn't quit school.

_____

_____

6. Barb married Tom. Because of him, she moved to Toronto.

_____

_____

7. Barb knew how to speak French and Spanish. That's why she got a job with an airline.

_____

_____

8. Jan got pneumonia. That's why she moved to Arizona.

_____

_____

9. Jan moved to Arizona. That's where she learned to ride a horse.

_____

_____

10. There wasn't birth control years ago. My grandmother had twelve children.

_____

_____

How did different people and events change _your_ life? Write three hypothetical conditionals about your own past.

11. _____

_____

12. _____

_____

13. _____

_____

▶ **EXERCISE 5**   _(Focus 3, page 367)_

Write hypothetical conditionals based on the following sentences.

▶ **EXAMPLE:** I didn't know that you needed me, so I went home.

If I had known that you needed me, I wouldn't have gone home.

1. I didn't give her the message because I didn't see her.

_____

_____

2. I wasn't able to go with you last weekend because I didn't have any money.

_____

_____

3. I didn't know you were in the hospital, so I didn't visit you.

_____

_____

4. We got into trouble because we broke the law.

_____

5. I didn't know we were going to be so late, so I didn't call you.

_____

_____

6. I ate the cookies because they were there.

_____

_____

7. You made a lot of mistakes because you weren't careful.

_____

_____

8. Lexi wasn't at the meeting, so we weren't able to solve the problem.

_____

_____

9. I didn't have a car, so I took the subway.

_____

_____

10. You told me the news, so I knew.

_____

_____

▶ **EXERCISE 6**   *(Focus 4, page 371)*

Three men have proposed to Eva. She doesn't know whether she should marry Mack, Sato, or Travis. The following are predictions about her life. Make future conditional sentences using *if* and the verbs below.

▶ **EXAMPLE:** marry Sato → move to Tokyo

If she marries Sato, she'll move to Tokyo. _____

SATO = JAPAN

1. move to Tokyo → have to learn Japanese _____

_____

2. learn Japanese → be the first one in her family to learn another language _____

_____

MACK = HOMETOWN

3. marry Mack → stay in Fremont, her hometown _____

_____

4. live in Fremont → not have to learn another language _____

_____

5. not leave Fremont → her life will not change very much _____

_____

TRAVIS = $$

6. marry Travis → be rich _____

_____

7. live in a mansion → feel like a princess _____

_____

8. not feel like herself → lose control over her life _____

_____

9. marry Sato or Travis → her life will be more exciting _____

_____

10. not get married → not have to worry about this _____

_____

▶ **EXERCISE 7**   *(Focus 5, page 373)*

Make future conditional sentences by completing the following. Be careful with punctuation.

1. If the rain stops soon _____

_____

2. My teacher will become angry if _____

_____

3. If people stop fighting wars _____

_____

4. I will say "you're welcome" if _____

_____

5. If you go barefoot _____

_____

6. I will leave the tip if _____

_____

7. If you don't stop that _____

_____

8. Oh, darling, if you leave me _____

_____

9. If I never see you again _____

_____

10. I'll be very happy if _____

_____

▶ **EXERCISE 8**   *(Focus 5, page 373)*

Complete this crossword puzzle. If you need help, ask a native speaker of English.

SUPERSTITIONS

ACROSS

1. _____ never strikes twice in the same place.
9. U.S. government organization that regulates airlines
10. One (Spanish)
12. If you hurt yourself, you say, "_____!"
14. The front of your leg between the ankle and the knee (plural)
15. If your job is to create good impressions of an organization with the public, then you work in _____. (abbreviation)
16. If a kitten is hungry, it _____ s.
18. If you go to Hawaii, you will be welcomed with a _____ around your neck.

19. If your name was Adam, you lived with Eve in the Garden of _____.

21. My sister was hurt at work, so she _____ the company because they didn't have any safety regulations.

22. If you pass under a ladder, you will have _____ luck.

23. If you want someone to go away, tell him to take a _____.

25. All right

27. Same as 6 Down

30. I made a wish on a falling star, but it hasn't come true _____.

31. North Carolina (abbreviation)

32. If you _____ salt, throw some of it over your shoulder to avoid bad luck.

33. Blood type

34. If the score is 2-2, we call it a _____.

36. If you nail a _____ over your door, it will bring you good luck.

DOWN

2. You will have bad luck _____ you open an umbrella indoors.

3. If it's not a liquid or a solid, it's a _____.

4. If you think something is funny, you say _____.

5. Religious sisters

6. If you want a green card, you will need to apply for one at the _____ office. (abbr.)

7. If you don't want any, just say "_____, thank you."

8. For good luck on her wedding day, a bride needs _____ old, _____ new, _____ borrowed, and _____ blue.

11. _____ 13th is an unlucky day. (2 words)

13. Marry

15. Urinate (slang)

17. If you are gone for fourteen days, it'll be two _____ that I won't see you.

18. You will be _____ if you find a four-leaf clover.

20. You will have bad luck if a black _____ passes in front of you.

24. If a company is incorporated, it will have this abbreviation at the end of its name.

26. Prefix meaning *air, gas,* or *aviation.*

28. Gorillas and monkeys

29. If you like light beer, then you probably won't like _____. (plural)

32. If you want to show respect to a man, you can call him "_____."

34 & 35. Opposite of *from*

Put a check (✓) next to the sentences that are hypothetical (the situation probably won't happen).

1. ___ I would move to Idaho if I won the lottery.

2. ___ If I don't find a job here, I'm going to move to Idaho.

3. ___ If Peggy were tall, she wouldn't have to look up at people.

4. ___ Tom's going to marry Barb if he gets a promotion.

5. ___ Tom would marry Barb if he made more money.

6. ___ We wouldn't have these problems if we spoke Japanese.

7. ___ If you go to Japan, you'll be able to practice your Japanese.

8. ___ I won't go with you if you wear that outfit.

9. ___ If they don't pay him more, he'll quit his job.

10. ___ Bob would quit his job if the company transferred him.

Use the words in the following list to complete the factual-conditional sentences below.

ask for a doggy bag	make a reservation
ask for the check	order an appetizer
ask for the manager	order another round
don't eat your food in the restaurant	the service is all right
like it cooked very little	want more coffee

1. If you're planning to go to a popular restaurant, you _____

2. You order takeout if you _____

3. When you buy everyone at your table a drink, you _____

4. You ask for a refill if you _____

5. If you want to eat something before the main course (or entrée), you _____

6. You order your meat rare if you _____

7. When you are ready to pay, you _____

8. If you want to take the rest of your meal home, you _____

9. You leave the server a 15 percent tip if _____

10. When you have a complaint, you _____

▶ **EXERCISE 11**　　*(Focus 6, page 375)*

Match the following to make complete sentences.

1. If you make something up, _____

2. When you make believe, _____

3. If you make dinner, _____

4. You talk when you _____

5. If you make off with something, you _____

6. Something is logical when it _____

7. If you make something over, _____

8. When you're successful, you've _____

A. it's renovated, or like new.
B. made it.
C. make a speech.
D. makes sense.
E. you pretend.
F. steal.
G. you're lying.
H. you cook.

▶ **EXERCISE 12**　　*(Focus 7, page 376)*

Use the words in the following list to complete the sentences below.

he might have died
I call the doctor today
I felt a lump in my breast
I hadn't quit smoking years ago
I might have gotten seriously ill

I had the flu
I see anything out of the ordinary
the doctors hadn't cured her cancer
you have the chills

1. I would call my doctor immediately if _____

2. If my father hadn't called 911 as soon as he did, _____

3. I will call my doctor and make an appointment if _____

4. I may not get an appointment for a couple of weeks if _____

5. I might have gotten bronchitis or lung cancer if _____

6. If I hadn't been vaccinated, _____

7. I might stay in bed and call in sick if _____

8. You may have a fever if _____

9. My mother wouldn't be alive today if _____

EXERCISES FOR THE TOEFL® TEST

Units 22–25

Choose the *one* word or phrase that best completes each sentence.

1. My aunt is going to _____ this evening. Would you like to meet her?
    (A) come over   (C) run into
    (B) came over   (D) drop me in on

2. Have I _____ your aunt before?
    (A) run into   (C) run her into
    (B) ran into   (D) looked up

3. No, I'm sure you haven't. If you _____ her before, you _____ her.
    (A) met . . . remember   (C) have met . . . would have remembered
    (B) had met . . . would remember   (D) had met . . . would remembered

4. My aunt is a very _____ person; she has had many _____ life experiences.
    (A) entertained . . . excited   (C) entertaining . . . exciting
    (B) entertained . . . exciting   (D) entertaining . . . excited

5. If her health _____ better, she _____ still be having exciting adventures.
    (A) was . . . will   (C) were . . . would
    (B) were . . . would have   (D) was . . . would have

6. She is an anthropologist. She is _____ diverse cultures.
    (A) interesting in   (C) interested of
    (B) interested in   (D) interesting of

7. My aunt collects artifacts from many different cultures. She never _____ .
    (A) throw anything away   (C) throws anything up
    (B) throws out anything   (D) throws away

8. She has a collection of things that _____ the healing ceremonies of different cultures.
    (A) are used by   (C) are used in
    (B) is used   (D) used by

9. She has written a book about healing plants. It _____ next year.
- (A) will publish
- (B) is going to be published
- (C) was published
- (D) is published

10. She has eaten herbs _____ jungle natives.
- (A) grown up
- (B) grew by
- (C) grow by
- (D) grown by

11. Some of the things she has eaten look _____ me.
- (A) disgusting to
- (B) disgusted by
- (C) disgusted to
- (D) disgusting by

12. If we _____ lucky, she _____ some of the things she has collected over the years to show us.
- (A) were . . . will bring
- (B) was . . . would bring
- (C) are . . . would bring
- (D) are . . . will bring

13. She also has an excellent collection of wooden carvings _____ North American Indians.
- (A) is made by
- (B) make by
- (C) are being made by
- (D) made by

14. If I _____ the opportunity, I _____ with my aunt on her expedition to the South American jungles last year.
- (A) had had . . . would have gone
- (B) have . . . will go
- (C) had . . . will go
- (D) had have . . . would have gone

Identify the *one* underlined word or phrase that must be changed for the sentence to be grammatically correct.

15. Marcia gets out very early, before sunrise, so when she gets dressed, it's still dark.
      A   B   C   D

16. This morning she must have been very tiring when she put on her clothes.
                     A   B   C   D

17. As usual, Marcia was picked up at 6:30 and was drived to work by her friend.
                      A   B   C   D

18. Marcia was giving a complicating presentation at work. She noticed that everyone
                              A
seemed very amused by the presentation.
   B   C   D

19. Marcia was confused and surprised for her coworkers' response because there was
                          A   B   C
nothing amusing about the presentation.
        D

20. Soon she finded out what was so amusing about her presentation.
           A   B   C   D

21. She realized she was wearing a blue shoe on her left foot and a brown shoe on her right
**A**

foot. Because it had been so dark in the morning, she had put away different shoes.
**B**$$**C**$$**D**

22. If she had paid more attention in the morning, she would of put on the correct shoes.
**A**$$**B**$$**C**$$**D**

23. She was embarrassing by her mistake, but she thought it was funny too.
**A****B**$$**C**$$**D**

24. If I was Marcia, I would be more careful in the morning.
**A****B****C****D**

25. One of her coworkers had a camera, so a picture of Marcia's feet with the two different
**A**$$**B**

shoes were taken.
**C****D**

26. Marcia's coworkers wouldn't let her forget about the different shoes. The photo of
**A**$$**B**

Marcia's feet was hanged on her office door.
**C****D**

27. Even if she lives to be 100 years old, Marcia would not forget that day.
**A****B**$$**C**$$**D**

28. She might had escaped all of the jokes if she were a more serious person.
**A****B****C**$$**D**

29. But Marcia likes to cheer up people with jokes, even if she is been teased by her
**A**$$**B**$$**C**$$**D**

coworkers.